SUPERNATURAL FINANCES

CONFERENCE STUDY NOTES

DR. KEVIN L. ZADAI

Dr. Kevin L. Zadai

SUPERNATURAL FINANCES

ı

ISBN 13 TP: 978-1-6631-0005-4

DR. KEVIN L. ZADAI

Dedication

I dedicate this book to the Lord Jesus Christ. When I died during surgery and met with Jesus on the other side, He insisted that I return to life on the earth and that I help people with their destinies. Because of Jesus's love and concern for people, the Lord has actually chosen to send a person back from death to help everyone who will receive that help so that his or her destiny and purpose is secure in Him. I want You, Lord, to know that when You come to take me to be with You someday, it is my sincere hope that people remember not me, but the revelation of Jesus Christ that You have revealed through me. I want others to know that I am merely being obedient to Your heavenly calling and mission, which is to reveal Your plan for the fulfillment of the divine destiny for each of God's children.

Acknowledgments

In addition to sharing my story with everyone through the books *Heavenly Visitation: A Guide to the Supernatural, Days of Heaven on Earth: A Guide to the Days Ahead, A Meeting Place with God, Your Hidden Destiny Revealed, Praying from the Heavenly Realms: Supernatural Secrets to a Lifestyle of Answered Prayer, and The Agenda of Angels,* the Lord gave me a commission to produce this book, *Supernatural Finances.* This book addresses some of the revelations concerning the areas that Jesus reviewed and revealed to me through the Word of God and by the Spirit of God during several visitations. I want to thank everyone who has encouraged me, assisted me, and prayed for me during the writing of this work, especially my spiritual parents, Dr. Jesse Duplantis and Dr. Cathy Duplantis. Special thanks to my wonderful wife Kathi for her love and dedication to the Lord and to me. Thank you, Sid Roth and staff, for your love of our supernatural Messiah, Jesus. Thank you, Dr. Janet Kline, for the wonderful job editing this book. Special thanks, as well, to all my friends who know about Supernatural Finances and how the to operate in them for the next move of God's Spirit!

Contents

DR. KEVIN L. ZADAI

Introduction

Through knowledge of His Word, it is possible for every Christian to have a great understanding of the nature of the Lord and of His ways. I often wonder how some Christians appear to God Almighty when, without having learned of Him through His Word, and while completely lacking crucial and essential understandings of Him, they try to interpret His ways. Without true knowledge of the Lord, knowledge that is easily accessed by reading of Him in the Bible, Christians often assume they know Him when they have almost no understanding, whatsoever, of His ways.

God has graciously revealed Himself through His Word in many avenues. One way that He reveals Himself is through His spoken Word. A second way that He reveals Himself is through His written Word. A third way that He reveals Himself is through His incarnate Word. When I met Jesus face-to-face, He clearly proved Himself to be complete in all three of these elements: He is the spoken Word, He is the written Word, and He is the incarnate Word. All three of these facets of the Word are encapsulated into one Person.

God has a strong personality. In every situation and in every circumstance, whatever our Father, the Holy Spirit, and Jesus have determined and agreed will always take precedence. The Holy Trinity will never be usurped or overtaken by anything other than what Jesus, the Father, and the Holy Ghost have agreed. The Trinity will never allow that to happen. God spoke all that was ever intended for mankind. And, after He spoke those intents for mankind, He took care to ensure that His plan for mankind was written down. Therefore, He has taken great care to reveal His plan to His own in His Word. Christians need to avail themselves of the revelation within the Word so they begin to understand the Lord more completely.

Because man sinned and disobeyed God, we now live in a fallen world that needs a savior. Jesus came in the flesh to demonstrate the Father's personality toward us. That personality is one of the purest love that has ever existed. I am honestly at a loss of words to describe how mankind sometimes is so presumptuous as to judge God through eyes of a fallen world. I am also at a loss for words to describe how mankind sometimes is so presumptuous to judge God through the eyes of the broken system of that fallen world. People continue to judge God in this way, completely oblivious to the fact that they do not have any correct understanding or any evidence of the ways of the Lord or even have basic informational truth concerning the Lord. The religious ideas of this fallen world create such a misrepresentation of the Lord. People often fail to realize the truth concerning the Lord that can be gained through knowledge of the Word of God.

When I met with Jesus, I told Him, face-to-face, that He was the most misrepresented Person on the earth. Most of mankind's perception of Him was not anything close to an accurate description of the true Savior Who loves us far beyond what we could ever ask or think. I want to explain to everyone how much better Jesus is in reality than anyone could ever imagine. Jesus told me how the enemy tries to sidetrack people away from their God-given destiny. As He explained the strategies of the enemy that are meant to distract us from our eternal destinies, I began to realize the actual depth of how different Jesus is in truth than the Person whom most people perceive.

Every one of our destinies are written down in a book in Heaven. I saw that the Holy Spirit is sent to lead every one of us into all truth. Part of this truth is exceedingly important to our victory in life, and that part of truth that is essential to victory is this fact: God wants His people to prosper. It was easy to understand how the enemy does not want the revelation of prosperity to be readily received by Christians. If His children knew the importance of prosperity, according to the way the Lord has predetermined that prosperity come forth to ensure victory for His people in life, Christians would understand the vital need to have prosperity. They would begin to grasp the extent of how they are to control the wealth of the world. The control of the wealth of the world is essential for the Kingdom of God to accomplish its task to prepare the people of the earth for the Lord's Second Coming and to prepare them for the great End-time Harvest of souls into God's Kingdom. Although the Gospel is free to all whom will receive it, it does take great finances to spread the Good News of Jesus in the earth. People must go, and in going, there are many costs, and one of the costs is that of finances.

Jesus showed me that the Spirit of God would begin to lead people into prosperity if they would yield to the will of God for their life. However, the yielding requires having the right motive. The motive of pursuing the wealth just to obtain wealth is a corrupt goal. Financial prosperity for the Kingdom's sake is the goal that encompasses the right motive. Those who seek financial prosperity for the building of the Kingdom of God will reach the goal that the Lord set. However, those seeking financial wealth merely for obtaining wealth will not reach the goal that the Lord set. The Spirit of God desires to reach those without Christ of this world with the

SUPERNATURAL FINANCES

Good News of Jesus. He therefore, very passionately, desires to lead His people into the truth concerning *Supernatural Finances.*

When I met with Him, Jesus focused upon this truth: every Christian must permit the Holy Spirit to take the lead in his or her life. When Christians permit the Lord to freely lead them, they will definitely be led to enter into prosperity in every area of life. That prosperity will not only be prosperity that pertains to the area of money. Jesus wants every Christian to understand that He will never limit anyone; it is His desire that every Christian will fulfill his or her destiny in Him. Simply put, Jesus desires to finance this last great End-time Harvest with unlimited supernatural provision from Heaven. Jesus plans to provide that unlimited supernatural provision from Heaven for anyone who can be trusted with wealth. Trusting those who will handle that wealth to support the last great revival on earth is part of the plan to prepare the earth before the Lord returns.

My personal recommendation is that every Christian learn of God's desire to place supernatural finances into his or her hands! If a Christian can pass this money test, then he or she will be ready to become an essential part of the End-time Harvest. It is my desire that every Christian who desires to be a part of God's plan for this time on earth must take the necessary steps to become blessed with supernatural finances. Then, each Christian who seeks to become blessed with supernatural finances so that he or she can help to fund the final move of God will be eligible to join me in full participation for preparation for the End-time Harvest before the return of our Lord to the earth!

Dr. Kevin L. Zadai

Chapter 1

The Almighty's Word

*It is the same with my word. I send it out, and it
always produces fruit. It will accomplish all I want it to, and it will prosper
everywhere I send it. Isaiah 55:11*

DISCUSSION:

No one in all creation can compare to the Lord, God Almighty. He always was, He always is, and He is always to come. The Apostle John wrote, "Each of these living beings had six wings, and their wings were covered all over with eyes, inside and out. Day after day and night after night they keep on saying, "Holy, holy, holy is the Lord God, the Almighty—the one who always was, who is, and who is still to come (Revelation 4:8 NLT)." The Lord surely has established His will for your life. He has good plans for you as you seek Him with all your heart.

THE ESTABLISHMENT OF HIS WORD

◈ **Psalm 33:11** (NLT) "But the Lord's plans stand firm forever; his intentions can never be shaken."

- o We should always remind ourselves that God has plan, and must acknowledge that those plans are to be in effect forever.
- o Whatever God has determined in His heart to accomplish, that is what He will accomplish.
- o He has established His Throne and will always have a foundation that will not be shaken.

Discuss God's plans and intentions for your life concerning supernatural provision:

_____

_____

_____

_____

_____

_____

_____

_____

_____

◈ **Jeremiah 1:12** (AMP) "For I am alert and active, watching over My word to perform it."

- o The Lord has spoken some things over us that are very powerful.
- o The Lord is continually looking over His Word.
- o Whatever it is that the Lord has spoken, He is aware of what He has said, and He is watching over His words to make sure that they comes to pass.
- o As believers, we must release God so that He is able to accomplish all that He intends for us to receive.
- o Remember that nothing is impossible to those who believe (See Mark 9:23).

What is the Holy Spirit saying to you about the Lord watching over His Word concerning supernatural provision?

_____

_____

_____

_____

_____

_____
_____
_____
_____

◈ **Isaiah 40:8** (NLT) "The grass withers, the flower fades, but the word of our God stands forever."

- o We must be fully convinced that God is able to outlast anything or anyone.
- o Everything natural will fade away, but God Himself will endure forever.
- o Every word that God speaks are spiritual words that are everlasting.

What God says is permanently in effect forever. What do you perceive He has said about you concerning supernatural provision?

_____
_____
_____
_____
_____
_____
_____
_____
_____

◈ **Malachi 3:6** "For I am the Lord, I do not change."

- o Because the Lord is everlasting, whatever He says is also everlasting.
- o His words do not change because he is everlasting and full truth.
- o The Lord has not changed concerning what He has spoken about you, nor does He change concerning what He has spoken over you.
- o God's truth is permanent.

What does the phrase, "I Change not" mean to you personally for your life in relation to supernatural provision?

_____
_____
_____
_____
_____
_____

_____
_____

◆ **Hebrews 13:8** "Jesus Christ is the same yesterday, today, and forever."
  ○ Jesus was the Preexistent One.
  ○ When He came to this earth, He came as the Son of Man.
  ○ Before Time began, He was the Son of God slain from the foundation of the world (see Revelation 13:8).

_____
_____
_____
_____
_____
_____
_____
_____

◆ The Lord is known for proclaiming truth.
◆ The Lord's throne is based on *absolute truth.*
◆ Psalms 89:14 says "Righteousness and justice are the foundation of your throne. Unfailing love and truth walk before you as attendants."
◆ Anything and everything that the Lord speaks is in the Realm of Truth and is also binding forever.
◆ God always means what He says.

What does the Holy Spirit say concerning truth that is *Absolute?*

_____
_____
_____
_____

◆ **The apostle Paul said, "'Eye has not seen, nor ear heard, nor have entered into the heart of man the things which *God has prepared for those who love Him.*' But God *has revealed* them to us through His Spirit. For the Spirit searches all things, yes, the deep things of God" (1 Cor. 2:9-10).**
◆ Every Christian must establish a deep trust in our heavenly Father's love for him or her, as well as a deep trust in the Lord's ability to accomplish all that concerns us.

◈ Each of us must have revelation concerning this truth before we can advance to success in every area of our lives.

◈ God desires that our lives be successful, especially for His Kingdom.

What is the meaning for each Christian, do you suppose, when the Spirit says we must know the deep things of God?

_____
_____
_____
_____
_____
_____

The Lord, by His Spirit, is saying to you,
"I love you with an everlasting love. I, long ago, thought of you and breathed you into your mother's womb. I wrote a book about your days before one day came to pass! You are in My arms and you are in My plans. I will see to it that all My plans for you come to pass.
If only you will trust in Me! (See Psalm 139:16.)

Do you trust Him? What is the application of this prophecy in your life?

_____
_____
_____

Unveiling the Other Realm

◈ **In the spirit realm, the Lord is looking at the future of each Christian's life as if that future is His now!** Therefore, we must not worry or be concerned about the future.

◈ Our Father has planned something better for each of His children than anyone could ever plan for himself or herself.

◈ There are things that are planned for every Christian that the angels know, but they are hidden from each of us for the moment. I am amazed at the intricacy of God's ways and how wonderful His thoughts are toward us.

◈ The psalmist wrote, **"How precious also are Your thoughts to me, O God! How great is the sum of them! If I should count them, they would be more in number than the sand; when I awake, I am still with You" (Ps. 139:17-18).**

The Lord is wanting to unveil truth in your life. Keeping that truth in mind, what do you desire for your life?

_____
_____
_____
_____
_____
_____
_____
_____
_____
_____
_____
_____
_____
_____
_____
_____

The Word of Truth

DISCUSSION:

Jesus reminded His hearers constantly that the words that He spoke were what the Father was telling Him to speak. He also continually reminded everyone that His words were spirit and that they were life. Jesus was taking the heart of the Father from the spirit realm and making God's heart known in the physical realm. Jesus was able to make God known in the physical realm by speaking the Father's words, by acting those words out, and by healing humanity. Manifestation of the truth is very important when we speak about truth. In fact, we must not just believe, but we must speak what we believe also. The angels are activated by our words. So when we speak the truth, we are coordinating our words with the words that are being spoken in Heaven.

◆ The angels that are assigned to us will implement our words when they are spoken by the Spirit of God.

◆ God speaks those words forth because He is the Spirit of truth.

◆ Manifestation of the truth will come.

◆ The angels are on duty at this very moment to make manifestation of the Word of God and cause the truth to come forth into your life.

◆ The Son of God speaks, and we are set free!

What is the assignment of angels concerning words?

_____

_____

_____

_____

*Then Jesus said to those Jews who believed Him, "If you abide in **My word**, you are My disciples indeed. And you shall know the **truth**, and the **truth** shall make you free." They answered Him, "We are Abraham's descendants, and have never been in bondage to anyone. How can You say, 'You will be made free'?" Jesus answered them, "Most assuredly, I say to you, whoever commits sin is a slave of sin. And a slave does not abide in the house forever, but a son abides forever. Therefore if the Son makes you free, you shall be free indeed"* (John 8:31-36).

◆ The truth is ignited right now, as the Word of the Lord forms inside of you and creates a fire.

◆ Speak the truth of the Lord Jesus Christ from that fire that you possess within yourself, and then prepare yourself to watch what will happen.

◆ The angels will begin to minister for you at the very hour that you speak the truth of the Lord Jesus Christ!

What is the Holy Spirit saying to you concerning the fire of God?

_____

_____

_____

_____

_____

_____

_____

_____

DR. KEVIN L. ZADAI

Chapter 2

Understanding the Sacredness
of the Tithe

'And all the tithe (tenth part) of the land, whether the seed of the land or the fruit of the tree, is the Lord's; it is holy to the Lord (Leviticus 27:30).

DISCUSSION:

When God created the heavens and the earth, He rested on the seventh day. He set apart that one day of the week as holy, the seventh day. This seventh day was to be given back to the Lord for an offering so that man would therefore acknowledge the Lordship of God in life. When the Lord made the Garden of Eden, He gave mankind access to everything except the tree of knowledge of good and evil. This tree was only for Himself, it was not for mankind. When the Lord does something for people, He asks them to remember Him by giving back a portion. In asking that the people give back a portion, the Lord emphasizes to the people who are receiving that they must remember the source from which the blessings came. The Source that they must recognize is the Lord.

Jesus was the fulfillment of the law, therefore, He did not abolish it. "Don't misunderstand why I have come. I did not come to abolish the Law of Moses or the writings of the prophets. No, I came to accomplish the purpose of the law and the writings of the prophets. I tell you the truth, until heaven and earth disappear, not even the smallest detail of God's law will disappear until its purpose is achieved. Therefore, if you ignore the least commandment and teach others to ignore it also, you will be called the least in the Kingdom of Heaven. But anyone who obeys God's laws and teaches them will be called great in the Kingdom of Heaven (Matthew 5:17-19).

◆ Do not misunderstand why Jesus has come.

◆ Jesus did not come to abolish the Law of Moses, nor did He come to abolish the writings of the prophets.

◆ No, Jesus came to accomplish the purpose of the law and of the writings of the prophets. I tell you the truth, until heaven and earth disappear, not even the smallest detail of God's law will disappear until the purpose is fulfilled.

◆ If anyone ignores the least commandment and teaches others to ignore the least commandment also, he or she will be called the least in the Kingdom of Heaven.

◆ But anyone who obeys God's laws and teaches them will be called great in the Kingdom of Heaven.

What is the Holy Spirit saying in Matthew 5:17-19?

_____

_____

_____

_____

_____

_____

_____

_____

_____

_____

_____

_____

A DEEPER STUDY: Numbers 18:17-32 NLT.

1. "However, you may not redeem the firstborn of cattle, sheep, or goats. *They are holy and have been set apart for the Lord.* Sprinkle their blood on the altar, and burn their fat as *a special gift, a pleasing aroma to the Lord.* The meat of these animals will be yours, just like the breast and right thigh that are presented by *lifting them*

up as a special offering before the altar. <u>Yes, I am giving you all these holy offerings that the people of Israel bring to the Lord. They are for you and your sons and daughters, to be eaten as your permanent share</u>. This is an eternal and unbreakable covenant between the Lord and you, and it also applies to your descendants."

◈ *"They are holy and have been set apart for the Lord."*

_____
_____
_____
_____

◈ *"a special gift, a pleasing aroma to the Lord."*

_____
_____
_____
_____

◈ *lifting them up as a special offering before the altar.*

_____
_____
_____
_____

◈ *This is an eternal and unbreakable covenant between the Lord and you, and it also applies to your descendants."*

_____
_____
_____
_____

◈ *<u>Yes, I am giving you all these holy offerings that the people of Israel bring to the Lord. They are for you and your sons and daughters, to be eaten as your permanent share</u>.*

_____
_____

---

2. And the Lord said to Aaron, "You priests will receive no allotment of land or share of property among the people of Israel. *I am your share and your allotment.* As for the tribe of Levi, your relatives, I will compensate them for their service in the Tabernacle. Instead of an allotment of land, *I will give them the tithes from the entire land of Israel.*

 ◆ *"I am your share and your allotment."*

 ◆ "As for the tribe of Levi, your relatives, I will compensate them for their service in the Tabernacle."

 ◆ *"I will give them the tithes from the entire land of Israel."*

---

3. "From now on, no Israelites except priests or Levites may approach the Tabernacle. If they come too near, they will be judged guilty and will die. Only the Levites may serve at the Tabernacle, and they will be held responsible for any offenses against it. This is a permanent law for you, to be observed from generation to generation. *The Levites will receive no allotment of land among the Israelites, because I have given them the Israelites' tithes, which have been presented as sacred offerings to the Lord.*

<u>This will be the Levites' share.</u> That is why I said they would receive no allotment of land among the Israelites."

◈ ***"The Levites will receive no allotment of land among the Israelites, because I have given them the Israelites' tithes, which have been presented as sacred offerings to the Lord."***

_____
_____
_____
_____

◈ <u>This will be the Levites' share.</u>

_____
_____
_____
_____

1 Peter 2:5

Come and be his "living stones" who are continually being assembled into a sanctuary for God. For now you serve as holy priests, offering up spiritual sacrifices that he readily accepts through Jesus Christ.

4. The Lord also told Moses, "Give these instructions to the **_Levites:_** *When you receive from the people of Israel the tithes I have assigned as your allotment, give a tenth of the tithes you receive—a tithe of the tithe—to the Lord as a sacred offering.* The Lord will consider this offering to be your harvest offering, as though it were the first grain from your own threshing floor or wine from your own winepress. ***You must present one-tenth of the tithe received from the Israelites as a sacred offering to the Lord.*** This is the Lord's sacred portion, and you must present it to Aaron the priest. Be sure to give to the Lord the best portions of the gifts given to you.

◈ "Give these instructions to the **_Levites:_**

◆ When you receive from the people of Israel the tithes I have assigned as your allotment, give a tenth of the tithes you receive—a tithe of the tithe—to the Lord as a sacred offering.

_____
_____
_____
_____

5. "Also, give these instructions to the Levites: *When you present the best part as your offering, it will be considered as though it came from your own threshing floor or winepress.* **You Levites and your families may eat this food anywhere you wish, for it is your compensation for serving in the Tabernacle.** _You will not be considered guilty for accepting the Lord's tithes if you give the best portion to the priests._ **But be careful not to treat the holy gifts of the people of Israel as though they were common. If you do, you will die."** Numbers 18:17-32 NLT.

◆ **When you present the best part as your offering, it will be considered as though it came from your own threshing floor or winepress.**

_____
_____
_____
_____

◆ _You will not be considered guilty for accepting the Lord's tithes if you give the best portion to the priests._

_____
_____
_____
_____

◈ **But be careful not to treat the holy gifts of the people of Israel as though they were common. If you do, you will die."**

Revelation 20:6 NLT

Wonderfully blessed and holy are those who share in the first resurrection! The second death holds no power over them, but they will be priests of God and of the Christ. And they will reign as kings with Him a thousand years!

Explain what the Holy Spirit saying to you concerning this phrase, "They will be priests of God and of the Christ. And they will reign as kings with him a thousand years!"

Romans 5:17 NLT

For if by the trespass of the one (Adam), death reigned through the one (Adam), much more surely will those who receive the abundance of grace and the free gift of righteousness reign in [eternal] life through the One, Jesus Christ.

What is the Holy Spirit saying to you concerning this phrase, "…much more surely will those who receive the abundance of grace and the free gift of righteousness reign in [eternal] life through the One, Jesus Christ."?

_____

_____

_____

_____

_____

_____

_____

_____

_____

_____

_____

Luke 11:42 NLT

"What sorrow awaits you Pharisees! For you are careful to tithe even the tiniest income from your herb gardens, but you ignore justice and the love of God. You should tithe, yes, but do not neglect the more important things.

State what you believe the Holy Spirit is saying to you concerning this phrase, "…but you ignore justice and the love of God. **You should tithe, yes,** but do not neglect the more important things."

_____

_____

_____

_____

_____

_____

_____

_____

_____
_____
_____

This Melchizedek was king of the city of Salem and also a priest of God Most High. When Abraham was returning home after winning a great battle against the kings, Melchizedek met him and blessed him. Then Abraham took a tenth of all he had captured in battle and gave it to Melchizedek. The name Melchizedek means "king of justice," and king of Salem means "king of peace." There is no record of his father or mother or any of his ancestors—no beginning or end to his life. He remains a priest forever, resembling the Son of God.

Consider then how great this Melchizedek was. Even Abraham, the great patriarch of Israel, recognized this by giving him a tenth of what he had taken in battle. Now the Law of Moses required that the priests, who are descendants of Levi, must collect a tithe from the rest of the people of Israel, who are also descendants of Abraham. But Melchizedek, who was not a descendant of Levi, collected a tenth from Abraham. And Melchizedek placed a blessing upon Abraham, the one who had already received the promises of God. And without question, the person who has the power to give a blessing is greater than the one who is blessed.

The priests who collect tithes are men who die, so Melchizedek is greater than they are, because we are told that he lives on. In addition, we might even say that these Levites—the ones who collect the tithe—paid a tithe to Melchizedek when their ancestor Abraham paid a tithe to him. For although Levi was not born yet, the seed from which he came was in Abraham's body when Melchizedek collected the tithe from him. Hebrews 7:1-10 NLT

Who told Abraham to tithe to Melchizedek? Explain how this is even possible for Abraham to know before Moses was given the Law on Mt. Sinai concerning the Tithe.

_____
_____

_____
_____
_____
_____
_____
_____
_____

Malachi 3:10-12 "Bring all the tithes into the storehouse, that there may be food in My house, and try (test) Me now in this," says the Lord of hosts, "If I will not open for you the windows of heaven and pour out for you such blessing that there will not be room enough to receive it. "And I will rebuke the devourer for your sakes, so that he will not destroy the fruit of your ground, nor shall the vine fail to bear fruit for you in the field," says the Lord of hosts; and all nations will call you blessed, For you will be a delightful land," says the Lord of hosts."

- ◆ Bring all the tithes into the storehouse.
- ◆ That there may be food in My house, and try (test) Me now in this," says the Lord of hosts.
- ◆ I will open for you the windows of heaven and pour out for you such blessing that there will not be room enough to receive it.
- ◆ I will rebuke the devourer for your sakes, so that he will not destroy the fruit of your ground, nor shall the vine fail to bear fruit for you in the field," says the Lord of hosts.
- ◆ All nations will call you blessed.
- ◆ For you will be a delightful land," says the Lord of hosts."

Comment on the above verses concerning tithing, and discuss the terms: *test me now, windows of Heaven, and rebuke the devourer.*

_____
_____
_____
_____
_____
_____

Leviticus 27:30 "And all the tithe of the land...is the Lord's. It is holy to the Lord."

What is God speaking to you concerning holiness, as it relates to the tithe and supernatural provision?

_____
_____
_____
_____
_____
_____
_____
_____

Proverbs 3:9-10 "Honor the Lord with your possessions, And with the firstfruits of all your increase; So your barns will be filled with plenty, And your vats will overflow (Hebrew: burst open violently) with new wine."

What is the Holy Spirit saying to you concerning this promise that if you honor the Lord with your possessions and the firstfruits of all you increase that your barns will be filled with plenty and you vats will overflow with new wine?

_____
_____
_____
_____
_____
_____
_____
_____

The Sacredness of the Sabbath

"Remember the Sabbath (seventh) day to keep it holy (set apart, dedicated to God). Six days you shall labor and do all your work, but the seventh day is a Sabbath [a day of rest dedicated] to the Lord your God; on that day you shall not do any work, you or your son, or your daughter, or your male servant, or your female servant, or your livestock or the temporary resident (foreigner) who stays within your [city] gates. For in six days the Lord made the heavens and the earth, the sea and everything that is in them, and He rested (ceased) on the seventh day. That is why the Lord blessed the Sabbath day and made it holy [that is, set it apart for His purposes] (Exodus 20:8-11 AMPC).

It is interesting to note that Jesus provided with an explanation for the true intent of giving back one day a week as an offering to the Father. It was set apart as holy and we were to rest just as God did during His week of creation. "Then Jesus said to them, 'The Sabbath was made to meet the needs of people, and not people to meet the requirements of the Sabbath. So the Son of Man is Lord, even over the Sabbath' (Mark 2:27-28 NLT)!

Jesus is even Lord over the Sabbath. He taught us to give it back to the Lord and permits us to do good things, saving the lives of others. "Then he turned to his critics and asked, 'Does the law permit good deeds on the Sabbath, or is it a day for doing evil? Is this a day to save life or to destroy it?' But they wouldn't answer him (Mark 3:4 NLT)."

We are to honor God with our first fruits of everything. Tithing is just honoring God for what He has given us. Every supernatural provision comes from Him.

What is the application that the Holy Spirit may have for your life concerning the sacredness of the Sabbath?

_____
_____
_____
_____
_____
_____
_____

Chapter 3

Accessing Battle Strategies Concerning Giving and Receiving

There was a famine in the land...
Then Isaac sowed in that land (in spite of famine), and reaped
in the same year a hundredfold; and the Lord blessed him. The man began to
prosper, and continued prospering until he became very prosperous
(Genesis 26:12).

DISCUSSION:

The Lord God has a supernatural battle strategy concerning your giving and receiving in the Kingdom of God. We live in a system of that is taken over by the spirit of this world. Satan desires to keep everyone under his control by either giving them great wealth at the sacrifice of their eternal life with Jesus, or by keeping people in debt so that they never are free. The fact is that God is willing for all to prosper and be in good health. "Beloved, I pray that in every way you may succeed and prosper and be in good health [physically], just as [I know] your soul prospers [spiritually] (3 John 1:2).

SECRET BATTLE STRATEGIES

1. Romans 12:8 says, "If you have the grace-gift of encouragement, then use it often to encourage others. *If you have the grace-gift of giving to meet the needs of others, then may you prosper in your generosity without fanfare.* If you have the gift of leadership, be passionate about your leadership. And if you have the gift of showing compassion, then flourish in your cheerful display of compassion.

   ◈ It is clear that some people are meant to prosper for generosity's sake.
   ◈ We are all called to prosper in everything that we endeavor to do because God's will always causes us to succeed.
   ◈ Jeremiah 29:11 says, "For I know the plans I have for you," declares the Lord, "plans to prosper you and not to harm you, plans to give you hope and a future."

   What is the Holy Spirit saying to you concerning secret battle strategies?

   _____
   _____
   _____
   _____
   _____
   _____
   _____

2. Genesis 22:14: "And Abraham called the name of the place, The-Lord-Will-Provide (Hebrew: Jehovah-jireh)"

   ◈ God Almighty sees every need and wants to provide for each of His children.
   ◈ The Lord has the ability to fix anything for every one of His own.
   ◈ If Almighty God does not have that item to give for which one of His children may ask, He will create it! Our Lord is that powerful!

   What is the Holy Spirit saying to you?

   _____
   _____
   _____
   _____
   _____

_____
_____
_____

3. Deuteronomy 8:18: "And you shall remember the Lord your God, for it is He who gives you power to get wealth, that He may establish His covenant which He swore to your fathers, as it is this day. "

   ◈ The Lord God is the supreme authority of all creation.
   ◈ God gave a covenant, and He desires for every single one of His children to participate fully in that covenant.
   ◈ The covenant started with Abraham. Now the covenant is complete through Jesus Christ.
   ◈ One of the ways that God establishes His covenant is by giving His people the power to get wealth.

   What is the Holy Spirit saying to you concerning the power to get wealth and God's establishment of His covenant concerning this power?

   _____
   _____
   _____
   _____
   _____
   _____
   _____
   _____

4. Deuteronomy 15:6: "For the Lord your God will bless you just as He promised you; you shall lend to many nations, but you shall not borrow; you shall reign over many nations, but they shall not reign over you."

   ◈ God's plan for every Christian is prosperity to the point that not one of His own ever will have a need to borrow.
   ◈ The Lord wants to openly display His covenant to everyone through His people.
   ◈ One of the ways God does confirmation His promise of wealth is through the financial system.
   ◈ He intends that He, Himself, and no one else will be able to rule over any of His children.

What is the Holy Spirit saying to you concerning God's blessing and display of His covenant of wealth through your life and through who will reign over you?

_____
_____
_____
_____
_____
_____
_____

5. Deuteronomy 16:15: "...The Lord your God will bless you in all your produce and in all the work of your hands, so that you surely rejoice."

   ◆ The Lord will overcome you with goodness to the point that even the works of your hands will be blessed.
   ◆ This will cause you to have a great joy.
   ◆ Everything that you touch will prosper.

   What is the Holy Spirit saying to you concerning blessing your produce and your hands concerning your great joy and your prosperity?

_____
_____
_____
_____
_____
_____
_____

6. Joshua 1:8: "This Book of the Law (The Word of God) shall not depart from your mouth, but you shall meditate in it day and night, that you may observe to do according to all that is written in it. For then you will make your way prosperous, and then you will have good success."

◈ Remember to meditate on everything that God says.
◈ This is God's will for you every day.
◈ Put into action all that you believe.
◈ God promises to make your way prosperous, and then you will have good success.

What is the Holy Spirit saying to you concerning following God's law (Word) and its relationship to your prosperity and success?

_____
_____
_____
_____
_____
_____
_____

7. 2 Chronicles 26:5: "He (King Uzziah) sought God in the days of Zechariah, who had understanding in the visions of God; and as long as he sought the Lord, God made him prosper."

◈ You have understanding in the visions of God.
◈ Continue to seek the Lord and He will continue to prosper you.

What is the Holy Spirit saying to you concerning understanding the visions of the Lord and God's plan to prosper you?

_____
_____
_____
_____
_____
_____
_____

8. Psalm 1:1-3: "Blessed is the man (person) who walks not in the counsel of the ungodly, nor stands in the path of sinners, nor sits in the seat of the scornful; But his delight is in the law of the Lord, and in His law he meditates day and night. He shall be like a tree planted by the rivers of water that brings forth its fruit in its season, whose leaf also shall not wither; and whatever he does shall prosper."

   ◆ Walk with the Lord and seek His counsel.
   ◆ Delight yourself in the Word of God and meditate on it day and night.
   ◆ If you do not walk in the counsel of the unglodly, nor stand in the path of sinners, nor sit in the seat of the scornful, and delight in the law of the Lord, you will prosper and everything you put your hands to do will produce and flourish, just like the tree planted by the rivers of water.

   What is the Holy Spirit saying to you concerning listening to the counsel of the ungodly, standing in the path of sinners, sitting in the seat of the scornful, as compared to delighting oneself in the law of the Lord?

   _____
   _____
   _____
   _____
   _____
   _____
   _____
   _____

9. Psalm 9:9: "The Lord also will be a refuge and a high tower for the oppressed, a refuge and a stronghold in times of trouble."

   ◆ Remember that your God has a place for you to seek refuge.
   ◆ You can run to Him and hide in times of trouble.
   ◆ No one will be able to touch you.

   What is the Holy Spirit saying to you concerning God as our refuge, especially in times of trouble, and God's protection from harm that others may try to inflict upon you?

_____
_____
_____
_____
_____
_____
_____
_____

10. Psalm 23:1, 5-6: "The Lord is my shepherd; I shall not want (I shall not be in lack)... Verse 5-6: You prepare a table (feast) before me in the presence of my enemies; You anoint my head with oil; my cup runs over (abundance). Surely goodness and mercy shall follow me all the days of my life.

◈ The Lord is your good shepherd, and you shall be in need of nothing.
◈ The Lord will even set a table in the presence of your enemies and anoint you with abundance.
◈ Goodness and mercy shall follow you, as well as overcome you, all the days of your life.

What is the Holy Spirit saying to you concerning the Lord as your shepherd as well as provision, abundance, and goodness and mercy?

_____
_____
_____
_____
_____
_____
_____

11. Psalm 35:27: "Let them shout for joy and be glad, who favor my righteous cause; And let them say continually, "Let the Lord be magnified, Who has pleasure in the prosperity of His servant."

◈ God will show you favor for your righteous cause.

◆ Continually magnify Him, and He will confirm His covenant with you.
◆ He desires to prosper you, and it gives Him great pleasure to do so.

What is the Holy Spirit saying to you concerning God's favor in your righteous cause, your continual magnification of Him, the confirmation of His covenant with you, His desire to prosper you, and His pleasure in your prosperity?

_____

_____

_____

_____

_____

_____

_____

12. Psalm 36:8: "They (those who trust in God) are abundantly satisfied with the fullness of Your house, And You give them drink from the river of Your pleasures."

◆ Always remember to trust your God.
◆ When you trust in Him, He promises to abundantly satisfy with the fullness of His house.
◆ The Lord God will actually give you a drink from the river of pleasure.

What is the Holy Spirit saying to you concerning trusting in God, His promises to satisfy those of His house, and giving you good things from the river of pleasure?

_____

_____

_____

_____

_____

_____

13. Psalm 37:3-4: "Trust in the Lord, and do good; dwell in the land (the blessing), and feed on His faithfulness. Delight yourself also in the Lord, and He shall give you the desires of your heart."

◆ Continually trust in the Lord your God.
◆ Continually think about His faithfulness to you.
◆ Remember to take delight in the Almighty God.
◆ He is willing to give you the desires of your heart if you will allow Him to do so.

What is the Holy Spirit saying to you concerning trusting God, thinking about His faithfulness, delighting in the Lord, and His desire to give you the desires of your heart?

_____
_____
_____
_____
_____
_____
_____

14. Psalm 37:18-19: "The Lord knows the days of the upright, and their inheritance shall be forever. They shall not be ashamed in the evil time, and in the days of famine they shall be satisfied."

◆ Remember that God knows all your days.
◆ He will keep your inheritance forever.
◆ Your future is secure and nothing shall be lost, even in famine.

What is the Holy Spirit saying to you concerning God's knowledge of your days, your eternal inheritance, your life in evil times, and your satisfaction in the days of famine?

_____
_____

_____
_____
_____
_____
_____
_____

15. Psalm 37:25: "I have been young, and now am old; Yet I have not seen the righteous forsaken, nor his descendants begging bread."

◆ The Lord will continually watch over you and not leave you.
◆ Because of God's faithfulness, He will not allow you to stay in need.
◆ He will come to you provide for you.

What is the Holy Spirit saying to you concerning God's watch over you, His faithfulness to stay with you, and His provision for your need?

_____
_____
_____
_____
_____
_____
_____

16. Psalm 65:4: "Blessed is the man You choose, and cause to approach You, that he may dwell in Your courts. We shall be satisfied with the goodness of Your house, of Your holy temple."

◆ Lord is inviting us into His courts.
◆ We are considered His children.
◆ And His house we will be satisfied with every good thing.

What is the Holy Spirit saying to you concerning our invitation into the courts of the Lord, our stance as His own, and our satisfaction with every good thing?

_____
_____
_____
_____
_____
_____
_____

17. Psalm 65:11: "You crown the year with Your goodness, And Your paths drip with abundance."

◈ The path the Lord has chosen for you will prosper.
◈ The path that He chose for you drips with abundance

What is the Holy Spirit saying to you concerning the prosperity on the path that God has chosen for you?

_____
_____
_____
_____
_____
_____
_____

18. Psalm 66:12: "We went through fire and through water; But You brought us out to rich fulfillment (KJV - wealthy place)."

◈ Whatever it is that you have gone through, or whatever you may be going through at the present time, the Lord will bring you out and into His wealthy place.

◆ The Lord is faithful, and your trouble will be well worth it when you see His deliverance come.

What is the Holy Spirit saying to you concerning the Lord bringing you to a wealthy place, God's faithfulness, and the worth of your trouble when you see His deliverance arrive?

_____
_____
_____
_____
_____
_____
_____
_____

19. Psalm 68:6: "God sets the solitary in families; He brings out those who are bound into prosperity; But the rebellious dwell in a dry land."

◆ The Lord has adopted you.
◆ He takes His own out of bondage, and He places them in families.
◆ He brings you out into prosperity.

What is the Holy Spirit saying to you concerning your adoption, deliverance form bondage, placement in a family and prosperity, as well as what happens to those who are rebellious?

_____
_____
_____
_____
_____
_____
_____

20. Psalm 68:19: "Blessed be the Lord, Who daily loads us with benefits, the God of our salvation!"

❖ The Lord himself will reward you for your faithfulness to him.
❖ He will load you down with all kinds of benefits.
❖ You do not need to worry anymore.

What is the Holy Spirit saying to you concerning the rewards and benefits of the Lord when you are faithful, as well as your concern about such things in life?

_____
_____
_____
_____
_____
_____
_____

21. Psalm 84:11: "For the Lord God is a sun and shield; the Lord will give grace and glory; no good thing will He withhold from those who walk uprightly."

❖ The Lord is always with you as a sun and a shield.
❖ The Lord is merciful and will give you grace.
❖ He will allow you to experience his glory.
❖ He will not withhold anything from you because have walked upright before Him.

What is the Holy Spirit saying to you concerning the Lord as your sun and shield, the Lord who gives grace and glory, and the generosity of the Lord to those who walk uprightly before Him?

_____
_____

_____

_____

_____

_____

_____

22. Psalm 107:38: "He also blesses them, and they multiply greatly; And He does not let their cattle decrease."

◆ The Lord will continually bless you and allow you to multiply in his kingdom.
◆ Nothing will decrease, but instead, all will increase.

What is the Holy Spirit saying to you concerning His continual blessing, His multiplication in your life, and the influence of decrease compared to the influence of increase in your life?

_____

_____

_____

_____

_____

_____

_____

23. Proverbs 4:18: "But the path of the just is like the shining sun, that shines ever brighter unto the perfect day."

◆ Keep walking with the Lord and you will see your path getting brighter and brighter.
◆ The Lord is leading you to the brightness of his glory.
◆ He has the perfect day as your destination.

What is the Holy Spirit saying to you concerning your walk with Him and the brightness of His glory, as well as the perfect day as your destination?

_____
_____
_____
_____
_____
_____
_____

24. Proverbs 6:30: "People do not despise a thief if he steals to satisfy himself when he is starving. Yet when he is found, he must restore sevenfold."

◆ The enemy in your life has been caught.
◆ Satan must pay you back sevenfold.
◆ The Lord himself will take up your case and bring restoration and recompense.

What is the Holy Spirit saying to you concerning the enemy who has stolen when he is caught, the amount of return when he is caught, and the Lord's part in bringing restoration and increase to you?

_____
_____
_____
_____
_____
_____
_____

25. Proverbs 8:21: "That I may cause those who love me to inherit wealth, that I may fill their treasuries."

◆ The Lord will cause you to inherit wealth because you love wisdom.
◆ He promises to fill your treasuries.

What is the Holy Spirit saying to you concerning those who love Him and the inheritance of wealth to fill their treasuries?

_____
_____
_____
_____
_____
_____
_____

26. Proverbs 10:3: "The Lord will not allow the righteous soul to famish"

◆ Lord is watching over you.
◆ Jesus Christ has made you righteous and his sight.
◆ The father will not allow your soul to experience lack for long, He will restore you.

What is the Holy Spirit saying to you concerning His watching over you, your righteousness in His sight, the length of your soul experiencing lack and your restoration?

_____
_____
_____
_____
_____
_____
_____

27. Proverbs 10:22: "The blessing of the Lord makes one rich, and He adds no sorrow with it."

◆ The Lord desires to bless his children.

- When he blesses, he makes one rich.
- Making a person rich by the Lord does not come with any sorrow, just joy unspeakable.

What is the Holy Spirit saying to you concerning God's desire to bless you, His making you rich, and the element of sorrow that does not come with the wealth, but rather the bringing of joy unspeakable in His blessings of wealth to His own?

_____
_____
_____
_____
_____
_____
_____

28. Proverbs 10:24: "The fear of the wicked will come upon him, and the desire of the righteous will be granted."

- Whatever the wicked fears is going to come upon them, put perfect love casts out fear in your life.
- God will grant you the desires of your heart because you have been made righteous by Christ Jesus.

What is the Holy Spirit saying to you concerning what comes upon those who are wicked, as compared to what comes upon those with perfect love?

_____
_____
_____

What is the Holy Spirit saying to you concerning the granting of the desires of your heart because you have been made righteous by the blood of Jesus Christ?

_____

_____

_____

_____

_____

29. Proverbs 11:25 (NIV): "A generous man will prosper; he who refreshes others will himself be refreshed."

◈ You cannot outgive God.
◈ Learn to become generous at all times.
◈ A generous person will prosper.
◈ When you refresh someone, you can expect that God will make certain that you receive refreshment from heaven.

What is the Holy Spirit saying to you concerning the prosperity of a generous person, what happens when someone who refreshes others, and the return that you can expect?

_____

_____

_____

_____

_____

_____

30. Proverbs 13:22: "A good man leaves an inheritance to his children's children, but the wealth of the sinner is stored up for the righteous."

◈ Allow the Lord to prosper you so that you can leave an inheritance to your children.
◈ Remember that the sinner is literally making money for you, and he is storing it on your behalf.

What is the Holy Spirit saying to you concerning prosperity and the inheritance you leave for your children, as well as the money that sinners are making that will come to you?

_____
_____
_____
_____
_____
_____
_____

31. Proverbs 15:6: "In the house of the righteous is much treasure: but in the revenues of the wicked is trouble."

◆ The blood Jesus is made you righteous in the sight of God.
◆ In the house of the righteous there is much treasure.
◆ God is with you in your house and no trouble shall befall you.

What is the Holy Spirit saying to you concerning the treasure of the righteous, and trouble which will not come to you when God is with you?

_____
_____
_____
_____
_____
_____
_____

32. Proverbs 22:4: "By humility and the fear of the Lord (worship & reverence) are riches and honor and life."

◈ Love the Lord to give you riches by humbling yourself in reverence, and worship before him.
◈ The Lord will surely lift you up and promote you.

What is the Holy Spirit saying to you concerning having humility and fear of the Lord, worshiping and reverencing Him and riches, honor, and life?

_____
_____
_____
_____
_____
_____
_____

33. Proverbs 28:10: (KJV) "Whoso causeth the righteous to go astray in an evil way, he shall fall himself into his own pit: but the upright shall have good things in possession."

◈ The Lord will guide and protect you.
◈ You have nothing to fear.
◈ Because you are upright, you will have good things in your possession.

What is the Holy Spirit saying to you concerning anyone who causes the righteous to go astray, as compared to what will happen to those who are upright?

_____
_____
_____
_____
_____
_____
_____

34. Proverbs 28:20: "A faithful man shall abound with blessings..."

◈ You are faithful and He will reward you.
◈ You will abound with blessings

What is the Holy Spirit saying to you concerning the faithful man and the abundance of blessings?

_____
_____
_____
_____
_____
_____
_____

35. Proverbs 28:25: "He who is of a proud heart stirs up strife, but he who trusts in the Lord will be prospered."

◈ Continually trust the Lord and see Him prosper you.
◈ Do not allow strife to be stirred up, but rather continually remain humble in the sight of Almighty God.

What is the Holy Spirit saying to you concerning stirring up strife as compared to trusting in the Lord and remaining humble In His sight and the results that will follow?

_____
_____
_____
_____
_____
_____
_____

36. Ecclesiastes 5:19: "As for every man to whom God has given riches and wealth, and given him power to eat of it, to receive his heritage and rejoice in his labor-- this is the gift of God."

   ◈ Remember that God gives the power for every man to obtain wealth.
   ◈ God desires for you to rejoice in this gift that He has given.

   What is the Holy Spirit saying to you concerning the power to obtain wealth, rejoicing in your labor, the gift of God, and receiving that wealth?

   _____
   _____
   _____
   _____
   _____
   _____
   _____

37. Isaiah 1:19: "If you are willing and obedient, you shall eat the good (the best) of the land."

   ◈ God is guiding you along the way, and He wants you to obey His instructions.
   ◈ This obedience will allow you to participate in the best or wealthiest places in the land.

   What is the Holy Spirit saying to you concerning your willingness and obedience to Him as it relates to your receiving the best and wealthiest of the land?

   _____
   _____
   _____
   _____
   _____
   _____
   _____

38. Isaiah 30:23: "Then He will give the rain for your seed with which you sow the ground, and bread of the increase of the earth; it will be fat and plenteous. In that day your cattle will feed in large pastures."

◈ God is a God of increase in your life.
◈ Whatever you can trust God for, He will provide for.

What is the Holy Spirit saying to you concerning the God of increase in your life and your trusting the Lord for provision?

_____
_____
_____
_____
_____
_____
_____

39. Isaiah 43:18-21: "Do not remember the former things, nor consider the things of old. Behold, I will do a new thing, now it shall spring forth; shall you not know it? I will even make a road in the wilderness and rivers in the desert. To give drink to My people, My chosen. This people I have formed for Myself; they shall declare My praise."

◈ You are God's chosen.
◈ Your loving Heavenly Father has amazing plans for you.
◈ He can even make rivers appear in the desert.
◈ He has formed you for Himself.
◈ We will give Him praise for all that He has done when the new springs forth.
◈ He wants you to forget the past and enjoy what is coming.

What is the Holy Spirit saying to you concerning the former things and what He will do, you as His chosen, His plans for you, His provision, praising Him for His provision, and praising Him?

_____
_____
_____
_____
_____
_____
_____
_____

40. Isaiah 45:2-3 (Amplified Version): "I will go before you and level the mountains [to make the crooked places straight]; I will break in pieces the doors of bronze and cut asunder the bars of iron. And I will give you the treasures of darkness and hidden riches of secret places that you may know that it is I, the Lord, the God of Israel, Who calls you by your name."

◆ The Lord desires for you to be free.
◆ He is coming to help you and make your crooked places straight.
◆ He will break the bars that imprison you.
◆ He will show you where the secret treasures are located, and He will give those secret treasures to you.

What is the Holy Spirit saying to you concerning His intervention on your behalf as you follow His direction, His provision, His revelation of hidden treasures in secret places, and His desire for you to know that it is God who has knowledge of you?

_____
_____
_____
_____
_____
_____
_____

41. Isaiah 48:17: "Thus says the Lord, your Redeemer, the Holy One of Israel: "I am the Lord your God, Who teaches you to profit, Who leads you by the way you should go."

◈ The Lord teaches us to profit.
◈ He will lead you into all truth and prosper you in the way chosen for you.

What is the Holy Spirit saying to you concerning Who the Lord is in relationship to you, what He teaches you to prosper, and how He leads you in the path where you should go?

_____
_____
_____
_____
_____
_____
_____

42. Isaiah 51:3: "For the Lord will comfort Zion, He will comfort (Pity, Change) all her waste places; He will make her wilderness like Eden, and her desert like the garden of the Lord; Joy and gladness will be found in it, thanksgiving and the voice of melody."

◈ Your Heavenly Father comforts you.
◈ He will perform a miracle and cause you to flourish like the garden of God.
◈ Joy shall come as you give thanks for His faithfulness.

What is the Holy Spirit saying to you concerning God's comfort for you, His causing you to flourish, and what will be present in our lives when He makes provision for you?

_____
_____
_____
_____
_____
_____
_____

43. Isaiah 58:11: "The Lord will guide you continually, and satisfy your soul in drought, and strengthen your bones; you shall be like a watered garden, and like a spring of water, whose waters do not fail."

◈ The Lord promises to guide you continually and defeat your enemy.
◈ He will satisfy you in drought with springs of living water and they will not fail.
◈ God is with you forever.

What is the Holy Spirit saying to you concerning His guidance for you, the defeat of your enemy, His satisfaction for your life, and His continual presence?

_____
_____
_____
_____
_____
_____
_____

44. Jeremiah 29:11: "For I know the thoughts that I think toward you, says the Lord, thoughts of peace and not of evil, to give you a future and a hope."

◈ The Lord has plans for you to prosper and succeed.
◈ Thoughts concerning peace and not of anything evil.

What is the Holy Spirit saying to you concerning His plans for your peace and for your life, as well as for your future and for your hope?

_____
_____
_____
_____
_____
_____
_____

45. Jeremiah 33:9: "Then it shall be to Me a name of joy, a praise, and an honor before all nations of the earth, who shall hear all the good that I do to them; they shall fear and tremble for all the goodness and all the prosperity that I provide for it."

◆ God loves to advertise His goodness to the nations.
◆ He wants to prosper His people and provide for them.

What is the Holy Spirit saying to you concerning His goodness and the nations of the earth, and the reaction of those who hear all that He does in providing goodness and prosperity to his people?

_____
_____
_____
_____
_____
_____
_____

46. Joel 2:25-26: "So I will restore to you the years that the swarming locust has eaten, the crawling locust, the consuming locust, and the chewing locust...You shall eat in plenty and be satisfied, and praise the name of the Lord your God, Who has dealt wondrously with you; and My people shall never be put to shame."

◆ God is a God of restoration.
◆ He will repay what the enemy has stolen from you.
◆ He has dealt WONDROUSLY with you!
◆ You will never be put to shame.

What is the Holy Spirit saying to you concerning God's restoration for you, the repayment of what the enemy has stolen from you, His provision, your praise of Him, His wondrous dealings with His own, and the fact that His people will never be put to shame?

_____
_____
_____
_____

_____

_____

_____

47. Haggai 2:8: "The silver is Mine, and the gold is Mine,' says the Lord of hosts."

◈ Your Father God is rich and owns the precious metals of the earth.

What is the Holy Spirit saying to you concerning the wealth of the Lord?

_____

_____

_____

_____

_____

_____

_____

48. Zechariah 8:12: "For the seed shall be prosperous, the vine shall give its fruit, the ground shall give her increase, and the heavens shall give their dew. I will cause the remnant of this people to possess all these things."

◈ You are to increase in every way.

What is the Holy Spirit saying to you concerning the prosperity of your seed, the fruit of your vine, the increase of the ground, the dew of heaven, and His people's possession of these things?

_____

_____

_____

_____

_____

_____

_____

49. Malachi 4:2: "But to you who fear My name (worship-reverence) the Sun of Righteousness shall arise with healing in His wings; and you shall go out and grow fat like stall-fed calves."

◈ Fear the Lord and healing is coming.

What is the Holy Spirit saying to you concerning those who fear His name and worship and reverence Him and what will happen concerning their healing and growth?

_____

_____

_____

_____

_____

_____

_____

50. Matthew 6:33: "But seek first the kingdom of God and His righteousness, and all these things shall be added to you."

◈ Seek God's Kingdom first, and you will see that God will ensure that you have all you need.
◈ He is righteous, and you are to seek His righteousness with all your heart.
◈ As you continually seek the Lord, He will never fail to provide all things for you.

What is the Holy Spirit saying to you concerning seeking God's kingdom and righteousness first and with all your heart, and the addition of the things that will be added to you?

_____

_____

_____

_____

_____

_____
_____

51. Matthew 7:11: "If you then, being evil, know how to give good gifts to your children, how much more will your Father who is in heaven give good things to those who ask Him!"

◈ Your Heavenly Father loves you and wants to give you good gifts.
◈ There is no earthly father that exceeds the Heavenly Father in giving.

What is the Holy Spirit saying to you concerning God's provision for His children and how it compares to the giving of earthly fathers?

_____
_____
_____
_____
_____
_____
_____

52. Mark 10:28-30: "Then Peter began to say to Him, "See, we have left all and followed You." So Jesus answered and said, "Assuredly, I say to you, there IS no one who has left house or brothers or sisters or father or mother or wife or children or lands, for My sake and the gospel's, who shall not receive a hundredfold now in this time — houses and brothers and sisters and mothers and children and lands, with persecutions — and in the age to come, eternal life."

◈ There is a reward system for all that you give up to follow Jesus.
◈ In this life, you will receive a hundredfold.
◈ As well as all the good things, persecutions will come for this abundance and reward that you receive in this present life.

What is the Holy Spirit saying to you concerning the reward system for all that you give to the Lord, the return of your giving in this life, and the persecution that will accompany the reward you receive in this present life?

_____
_____
_____
_____
_____
_____
_____

53. Luke 6:38: Jesus said; "Give, and it will be given to you: good measure, pressed down, shaken together, and running over will be put into your bosom. For with the same measure that you use, it will be measured back to you."

   ◈ God has not forgotten all the gifts you have given.
   ◈ He will reward you according to how you have measured it out.
   ◈ Always be generous, and then you will be running over in the blessings that come to you.

What is the Holy Spirit saying to you concerning giving, generosity, the return that you will receive, and the measure that will come back to you?

_____
_____
_____
_____
_____
_____
_____

54. Luke 12:32 "Do not fear, little flock, for it is your Father's good pleasure to give you the kingdom."

◈ God desires to give you the Kingdom.
◈ He is excited for the provision that is coming to you.
◈ Do not fear. You are going to see your deliverance.

What is the Holy Spirit saying to you concerning fear, receiving God's kingdom, and the pleasure God receives from giving to you?

_____

_____

_____

_____

_____

_____

_____

55. John 8:32: "And you shall know the truth, and the truth shall make you free."

◈ Let the truth of God rule and reign in your life.
◈ Truth will set you free from any bondage.

What is the Holy Spirit saying to you concerning knowing the truth and what that knowledge will do for a person?

_____

_____

_____

_____

_____

_____

_____

56. John 10:10: "The thief does not come except to steal, and to kill, and to destroy. I (Jesus) have come that they may have life, and that they may have it more abundantly."

◈ It is time to label the enemy by his fruit and his mission.
◈ He only wishes to destroy you as a child of God.

◈ The father God has sent Jesus to give life to you, and to give life that is more abundant to you.

◈ Jesus' mission included the provision of abundant life for His own.

What is the Holy Spirit saying to you concerning the plan of the thief for your life as compared to the plan of Jesus for your life?

_____

_____

_____

_____

_____

_____

_____

57. John 16:23-24: "And in that day you will ask Me nothing. Most assuredly, I say to you, whatever you ask the Father in My name He will give you. Until now you have asked nothing in My name. Ask, and you will receive, that your joy may be full."

◈ Jesus clearly says that we can ask anything and we will receive it.

◈ You receive so that your joy can be full.

What is the Holy Spirit saying to you concerning asking Him for anything and the resulting joy that will come when He responds?

_____

_____

_____

_____

_____

_____

_____

58. Romans 8:16-17: "The Spirit Himself bears witness with our spirit that we are children of God, and if children, then heirs--heirs of God and joint heirs with Christ, if indeed we suffer with Him, that we may also be glorified together."

- ◆ We have the Holy Spirit within us that continually speaks of us as God's children.
- ◆ We are joint heirs with Jesus who bought us.
- ◆ We also must suffer with Him in order to be glorified with Him

What is the Holy Spirit saying to you concerning our status as children of God our state of being heirs, and our suffering with Him to be glorified with Him?

_____

_____

_____

_____

_____

_____

_____

59. Romans 8:32: "He who did not spare His own Son, but delivered Him up for us all, how shall He not with Him also freely give us all things?"

- ◆ God has not withheld His only Son.
- ◆ He will not withhold any good thing but will give us all things.

What is the Holy Spirit saying to you concerning God giving His own Son, and God's desire not to withhold anything from His children?

_____

_____

_____

_____

_____

_____

_____

60. 1 Corinthians 16:2 (Amplified Version): "On the first [day] of each week, let each one of you [personally] put aside something and save it up as he has prospered [in proportion to what he is given], so that no collections will need to be taken after I come."

◈ Paul had the church set aside the offerings in advance for his collection when he came.

◈ It was according to how must God had "prospered" them.

What is the Holy Spirit saying to you concerning laying aside offerings in advance and doing that act in accordance with how God prospered them?

_____

_____

_____

_____

_____

_____

_____

61. 2 Corinthians 8:9: "For you know the grace of our Lord Jesus Christ, that though He was rich, yet for your sakes He became poor, that you through His poverty might become rich."

◈ Consider that God sent Jesus back from the wealthiest place in creation to a fallen earth.

◈ He redeemed us back by the blood of Jesus so that we could become like Him in glory.

What is the Holy Spirit saying to you concerning the grace of Jesus, and His loss of riches to take poverty upon Himself so that we might become rich though His poverty?

_____

_____

_____

_____

_____

_____

_____

62. Ephesians 1:3: "Blessed be the God and Father of our Lord Jesus Christ, who has blessed [prospered] us with every spiritual blessing in the heavenly places in Christ."

◆ Our Heavenly Father has blessed us with every spiritual blessing in the Heavenlies.
◆ Never doubt that He is wanting you to grow and mature spiritually.

What is the Holy Spirit saying to you concerning the blessing of God's children with every spiritual blessing in heavenly places in Christ and our need to grow spiritually to maturity?

_____

_____

_____

_____

_____

_____

_____

_____

63. Ephesians 3:20: "Now to Him who is able to do exceedingly abundantly above all that we ask or think, according to the power that works in us."

◆ God can exceed you expectations.
◆ His great power is working in us.
◆ We are not capable of asking or thinking what God is able to do for us.

What is the Holy Spirit saying to you concerning how God is able to do things exceedingly abundantly above all we ask or above all we think?

_____

_____

_____
_____
_____
_____
_____

64. Philippians 4:19 (Amplified Version):"And my God will liberally supply (fill to the full) your every need according to His riches in glory in Christ Jesus."

◈ God has an abundant supply to help you be full all the time.
◈ Your every need is met through Him.
◈ It is according to His riches in the glory that our every need is fulfilled.

What is the Holy Spirit saying to you concerning God's supply in relation to our need and the source of that supply for us?

_____
_____
_____
_____
_____
_____
_____
_____

65. 1 Thessalonians 4:12: "That you may walk properly toward those who are outside, and that you may lack nothing."

◈ The Lord wants you to walk properly.
◈ The Lord wants you to be a witness of His goodness to those who are not yet in His kingdom, and His provision is a demonstration of how His own lack nothing!
◈ He wants you to lack nothing!

What is the Holy Spirit saying to you concerning our walk toward those who do not yet belong to His kingdom, and His provision so that His children lack absolutely no good thing?

_____
_____
_____
_____
_____
_____
_____

66. 1 Timothy 4:8: "For bodily exercise profits a little, but godliness is profitable for all things, having promise of the life that now is and of that which is to come."

 ◆ Godliness is profitable for everything.
 ◆ Godliness is profitable in this life presently, as well as in the life to come.

What is the Holy Spirit saying to you concerning the profitability of godliness for all things in this life and in the life to come?

_____
_____
_____
_____
_____
_____
_____

67. Hebrews 6:12: "Do not become sluggish (Lazy), but imitate those who through faith and patience inherit the promises."

 ◆ As a good soldier in Christ, we must not be lazy.
 ◆ We must model our lives after those who inherit the promises thorough faith and patience.
 ◆ In so doing, we also will inherit the promises of God.

What is the Holy Spirit saying to you concerning laziness, and our exercise of faith and patience to inherit the promises of God?

_____
_____
_____
_____
_____
_____
_____

68. James 1:25: "But he who looks into the perfect law of liberty and continues in it, and is not a forgetful hearer but a doer of the word, this one will be blessed in what he does."

◈ Continue to look into the word of God
◈ The Word gives you liberty.
◈ We always must remember what is given to us by the Word of God and diligently and continually practice the perfect law of liberty.
◈ We must not forget what God has said, and we must be sure to do what He has said to be blessed.
◈ We are then blessed by what we do because God is with us.

What is the Holy Spirit saying to you concerning looking continually into the law of God, continuing to walk in the law of God, hearing the law of God, doing the word of God, being blessed as a result of those actions, and God's presence with us?

_____
_____
_____
_____
_____

_____

_____

69. 3 John 2: "Beloved, I pray that you may prosper in all things and be in health, just as your soul prospers."

◆ The Lord is willing to prosper you.
◆ He prospers you in your health.
◆ He prospers you in your finances.
◆ He prospers you in your soul.
◆ In EVERYTHING, He wants to prosper you!

What is the Holy Spirit saying to you concerning your prosperity in all things and in health in relationship to how your soul prospers?

_____

_____

_____

_____

_____

_____

_____

Chapter 4

The Fear of the Lord and Giving

Therefore, having these promises, beloved, let us cleanse ourselves from all filthiness of the flesh and spirit, perfecting holiness in the fear of God. —2 Corinthians 7:1

DISCUSSION:

God desires gifts that are set apart as holy whenever we present anything to Him. He accepts any gift based on the condition of our heart when we offer the gift. When we prayerful consider what we are to give to Him, we are to check our motives and keep a clean heart and conscience toward giving because the giving of gifts to the Lord is a sacred activity.

Awesome respect and fear concerning our Heavenly Father will naturally cause anyone who gives a gift to Him to repent of any evil ways and to humble himself or herself under His mighty authority. Though He loves us, He still requires holiness. That means we must be set apart from the ways of the world. There is no holiness present when someone is joined to the evil ways of this earth. Therefore, our gifts must be sincerely given. They cannot be attached to any ungodly heart issues that would be judged as not acceptable. In the Book of Acts, we read of an example of how God views giving with a heart that lacks holiness and a motive that is not pure. A couple gave a gift to the church in Acts, but their gift was without holiness because they conspired together to be deceitful in their giving. There was really no need for this couple to be deceitful, other than their desire to appear to be seen as givers in front of the people of the church. There was no need to lie about their gift, but yet they lied, thereby truly deceiving only themselves, for God knows all things.

Now, a man named Ananias and his wife, Sapphira, likewise sold their farm. *They conspired to secretly keep back for themselves a portion of the proceeds.* So when Ananias brought the money to the apostles, *it was only a portion of the entire sale.* God revealed their secret to Peter, so he said to him, "Ananias, why did you let Satan fill your heart and make you think you could lie to the Holy Spirit? *You only pretended to give it all, yet you hid back part of the proceeds* from the sale of your property to keep for yourselves. Before you sold it, wasn't it yours to sell or to keep? And after you sold it, *wasn't the money entirely at your disposal?* How could you plot such a thing in your heart? *You haven't lied to people; you've lied to God!"*

The moment Ananias heard those words, he fell over dead. Everyone was terrified when they heard what had happened. Some young men came in and removed the body and buried him. Three hours later, his wife came into the room, with no clue what had happened to her husband. Peter said to her, "Tell me, were the two of you paid this amount for the sale of your land?" Sapphira said, "Yes, that's how much it was."

Peter told her, *"Why have you agreed together to test the Spirit of the Lord?* I hear the footsteps of those who buried your husband at the door—they're coming here to bury you too!" At that moment she dropped dead at Peter's feet. When the young men came in, she was already dead, so they carried her out and buried her next to her husband. *The entire church was seized with a powerful sense of the fear of God, which came over all who heard what had happened.*

◆ **They conspired to secretly keep back for themselves a portion of the proceeds.**
◆ **It was only a portion of the entire sale.**
◆ "Ananias, why did you let Satan fill your heart and make you think you could lie to the Holy Spirit? **You only pretended to give it all, yet you hid back part of the proceeds.**"
◆ **Wasn't the money entirely at your disposal? How could you plot such a thing in your heart?**
◆ **You haven't lied to people; you've lied to God!"**

◆ The moment Ananias heard those words, he fell over dead.
◆ Peter told her, **"Why have you agreed together to test the Spirit of the Lord?"**
◆ The entire church was seized with a powerful sense of the fear of God, which came over all who heard what had happened.

What is the Holy Spirit saying to you concerning giving and the condition of our heart that must show respect and reverential fear for the Lord with the right motivations and the demonstration of true holiness when a gift is given?

_____
_____
_____
_____
_____
_____

There are a number of promises that support the fact that the fear of the Lord is effective in one's life. In Psalm 25:12-13 it says, "Who is the man that fears the Lord? Him shall He teach in the way He chooses. He himself shall dwell in prosperity, and his descendants shall inherit the earth." The fear of the Lord allows these benefits to be manifested in your life:

◆ You will be taught the specific way that the Lord choses for you.
◆ You will dwell in prosperity.
◆ Your descendants will inherit the earth.

What is the Holy Spirit saying to you concerning the fear of the Lord and our instruction, our dwelling in prosperity, and the inheritance our descendants will receive?

_____
_____
_____
_____

Psalm 34:9-10 "Oh, fear the Lord, you His saints! There is no want (no lack) to those who fear Him. The young lions lack and suffer hunger; but those who seek the Lord shall not lack any good thing."

◈ You will be taught the specific way that the Lord choses for you.
◈ You will dwell in prosperity.
◈ Your descendants will inherit the earth.

What is the Holy Spirit saying to you concerning the fact that those who fear Him suffer no lack, as well as a promise of no lack for their descendants also?

Psalm 112:1-3 "Praise the Lord! Blessed is the man who fears the Lord (worship & reverence), who delights greatly in His commandments (His Word). His descendants will be mighty on earth; the generation of the upright will be blessed. Wealth and riches will be in his house, and his righteousness endures forever."

◈ You are blessed when you fear the Lord
◈ You who worship Him will find that your descendants will be mighty on the earth.
◈ Wealth and riches will be in your house.
◈ His Righteousness endures forever.

What is the Holy Spirit saying to you concerning the blessing of God to those who fear Him, the blessing upon the descendants of those who worship Him, wealth and riches in your house, and the enduring righteousness of those who worship Him?

_____

_____

_____

_____

_____

_____

Chapter 5

Giving to Those Who Cannot Repay You

"So, now, go and sell what you have and give
to those in need, making deposits in your account in heaven, an account that
will never be taken from you. Your gifts will become a secure and unfailing
treasure, deposited in heaven forever. Where you deposit your treasure,
that is where your thoughts will turn to—and your heart
will long to be there also." (Luke 12:33-34 TPT)

DISCUSSION:

Jesus tells us not worry about anything. He does not want us overburdened with the pressures of making money in order to live. He talks about the heavenly kingdom, a kingdom where one can make deposits during this life that translate additionally as deposits for the life to come.

> I repeat it: Don't let worry enter your life. Live above the anxious cares about your personal needs. People everywhere seem to worry about making a living, but your heavenly Father knows your every need and will take care of you. Each and every day he will supply your needs as you seek his kingdom passionately, above all else. So don't ever be afraid, dearest friends! Your loving Father joyously gives you his kingdom realm with all its promises! "So, now, go and sell what you

have and give to those in need, making deposits in your account in heaven, an account that will never be taken from you. Your gifts will become a secure and unfailing treasure, deposited in heaven forever. Where you deposit your treasure, that is where your thoughts will turn to—and your heart will long to be there also (Luke 12:29-34 TPT)."

- ◆ Don't let worry enter your life.
- ◆ Live above the anxious cares about your personal needs.
- ◆ Your Heavenly Father knows your every need.
- ◆ Your loving Father joyously gives you his kingdom realm with all its promises!
- ◆ Make deposits in your account in heaven, an account that will never be taken from you.
- ◆ Your gifts will become a secure and unfailing treasure, deposited in heaven forever.

What is the Holy Spirit saying to you concerning worry, your personal needs, God's knowledge of your needs, God's giving of His kingdom and His promises to you, and the making of accounts in Heaven that will never be taken from you?

_____
_____
_____
_____
_____
_____

What is the application concerning what is the Holy Spirit saying to you about worry, your personal needs, God's knowledge of your needs, God's giving of His kingdom and His promises to you, and the making of accounts in Heaven that will never be taken from you?

_____
_____
_____
_____
_____

SUPERNATURAL FINANCES

"Watch out! Don't do your good deeds publicly, to be admired by others, for you will lose the reward from your Father in heaven. When you give to someone in need, don't do as the hypocrites do—blowing trumpets in the synagogues and streets to call attention to their acts of charity! I tell you the truth, they have received all the reward they will ever get. But when you give to someone in need, don't let your left hand know what your right hand is doing. Give your gifts in private, and your Father, who sees everything, will reward you. (Matthew 6:1-4 NLT).

◈ Do not do your good deeds publicly, to be admired by others.
◈ When you give to someone in need, do not do as the hypocrites do—blowing trumpets in the synagogues and streets to call attention to their acts of charity! I tell you the truth, they have received all the reward they will ever get.
◈ Give your gifts in private, and your Father, who sees everything, will reward you.

What is the Holy Spirit saying to you concerning doing good deeds publicly, the reward one does receive when their motivation is to call attention to their charity, and the reward God gives to those who do their giving privately?

_____
_____
_____
_____
_____
_____

What is the application for your life concerning doing good deeds publicly, the reward one does receive when their motivation is to call attention to their charity, and the reward God gives to those who do their giving privately?

_____
_____
_____
_____
_____

Then Jesus turned to his host and said, "When you throw a banquet, don't just invite your friends, relatives, or rich neighbors—for it is likely they will return the favor.

It is better to invite those who never get an invitation. Invite the poor to your banquet, along with the outcast, the handicapped, and the blind—those who could never repay you the favor. Then you will experience a great blessing in this life, and at the resurrection of the godly you will receive a full reward." Luke 14:12-14 TPT

◆ When you throw a banquet, do not just invite your friends, relatives, or rich neighbors—for it is likely they will return the favor.
◆ It is better to invite those who never get an invitation. Invite the poor to your banquet, along with the outcast, the handicapped, and the blind—those who could never repay you the favor.
◆ Then you will experience a great blessing in this life, and at the resurrection of the godly you will receive a full reward.

What is the Holy Spirit saying to you concerning inviting strangers who are poor and outcast who cannot return the favor and the blessing you will receive in this life and the reward you will receive at the resurrection?

_____
_____
_____
_____
_____
_____

What is the application for your life concerning giving to the poor and the rewards you will receive in this life and in the life to come?

_____
_____
_____
_____
_____

"And then those on his left will say, 'Lord, when did we see you hungry or thirsty and not give you food and something to drink? When did we see you homeless, or poorly clothed? When did we see you sick and not help you, or in prison and not visit you?'

"Then he will answer them, 'Don't you know? When you refused to help one of the least important among these my little ones, my true brothers and sisters, you refused to help and honor me.' And they will depart from his presence and go into eternal punishment. But the godly and beloved 'sheep' will enter into eternal bliss. " (Matthew 25:44-46 TPT)

◈ Lord, when did we see you hungry or thirsty and not give you food and something to drink? When did we see you homeless, or poorly clothed? When did we see you sick and not help you, or in prison and not visit you?'
◈ "Then he will answer them, 'Don't you know? When you refused to help one of the least important among these my little ones, my true brothers and sisters, you refused to help and honor me.'

What is the Holy Spirit saying to you concerning giving to those in need and the help that you give to them?

_____
_____
_____
_____
_____
_____

What is the application for your life concerning giving to those in need and the help that you give to them?

_____
_____
_____
_____
_____

Everything Counts

Every person counts, and everything you do with what God has given you counts. You are greatly rewarded for what you do in faith. Hebrews 11:6 was completely explained to me. When I was with Jesus, after I had died on the operating table, one of the lessons I learned from Him was that everything I do for Him counts.

◆ I was taught that if I did something in faith, it was recorded, and I was rewarded for that act of faith.

◆ Also, Jesus told me that even if I did something in His name, I was rewarded simply because I wanted to represent Him in an honorable way.

◆ Without faith, you cannot please God.

◆ I realize that it is not just enough to believe that God exists, but we must also believe that He a Rewarder of those who *diligently* seek Him.

◆ Jesus *has so much love for everyone*, but He needs for you to yield to the Holy Spirit and His faithful angels.

◆ His Faithful angels have been sent to expedite your destiny.

◆ He wants you to *tell* Him how much you trust Him every day.

◆ He wants you to *show* Him how much you trust Him every day in your actions.

What is the Holy Spirit saying to you concerning our actions in faith and their rewards, the importance of faith in pleasing God, doing things in His name and representing God in an honorable way, the rewards He gives for honoring Him in such giving, our need to recognize that He is a rewarder of those who diligently seek Him, the importance of yielding to the Holy Spirit and His faithful angels, the angels' role in expediting your destiny, the need to tell God that you trust Him daily, and the need to show God that you trust Him daily?

The Lord knows when you sacrifice. He asks, "What have you done?" This is so special, and He rewards you.

Immediate Obedience

Jesus told me during my *heavenly visitation* in 1992, that I had been faithful in all that He had ever asked me to do for Him. He mentioned that I am known in Heaven. He explained that Heaven speaks of me because of a character trait that is uncommon on the earth, and that is obedience without questioning the reasons for the need to do what is revealed. He said that it is rare to find someone such as I, who will always drop what I am doing, and immediately do whatever the Spirit is doing at the time. He said, "And you never even ask Me for an explanation; you just do it."

What is the Holy Spirit saying to you concerning obeying Him and refusing to question God's rationale behind His request that you do something?

_____

_____

_____

_____

_____

_____

Chapter 6

A Lesson on Kingdom Authority

*Now you understand that I have imparted to you all
my authority to trample over his kingdom. You will trample upon every
demon before you and overcome every power Satan possesses. Absolutely
nothing will be able to harm you as you walk in this authority. However, your
real source of joy isn't merely that these spirits submit to your authority,
but that your names are written in the journals of heaven and that
you belong to God's kingdom. This is the true source of your
authority (Luke 10:19-20 TPT)."*

DISCUSSION:

Jesus desires that everyone discern His authority. He went about doing good and healing everyone that was oppressed of the devil (See Acts 10:38). Jesus could do good only if those needing His help were able to discern His authority that is given from the Father God. The faith each one had in that authority would cause that person to receive from Him. He was the true Messiah, the Deliverer of Israel. However, the greatest faith encountered was not from the children of Israel! The greatest faith that Jesus encountered was from the Gentiles! One day Jesus found this type of faith in a Roman centurion.

> As Jesus went into Capernaum, a centurion came up to Him, begging Him [for help], and saying, "Lord, my servant is lying at home paralyzed, with intense and terrible, tormenting pain." Jesus said to him, "I will come and heal him." But the centurion replied to Him, "Lord, I am not worthy to have You come under my roof, but only say the word, and my servant will be healed. For I also am a man subject to authority

[of a higher rank], with soldiers subject to me; and I say to one, 'Go!' and he goes, and to another, 'Come!' and he comes, and to my slave, 'Do this!' and he does it." When Jesus heard this, He was amazed and said to those who were following Him, "I tell you truthfully, I have not found such great faith [as this] with anyone in Israel (Mathew 8:5-10 AMP).

- ◆ What Jesus says has just as much power as what He does.
- ◆ His word is enough to heal the sick.
- ◆ Jesus is the commander of your life.
- ◆ When Jesus gives a command that states that you are going to prosper, then you will surely prosper.
- ◆ When Jesus gives the command that you are healed, then you are surely healed.
- ◆ When Jesus gives the command that you are delivered then you are surely delivered.

What is the Holy Spirit saying to you concerning the power and what He says as compared to the power and what He does, how His word is enough to heal the sick, How He is commander of your life, how His command that you prosper will cause you to prosper, how His command that you are healed will cause you to be healed, and how His command that you are delivered will cause you to be delivered?

_____
_____
_____
_____
_____
_____

What is the application for your life concerning the power when Jesus speaks, the healing of the sick, His command over your life, and His command over your prosperity, healing, and deliverance?

_____
_____
_____
_____

_____

_____

THE LORD HAS COMMANDED BLESSINGS TO COME TO YOU FROM THE AUTHORITY OF HEAVEN!

1. Deuteronomy 28:2-8: "And all these blessings shall come upon you and overtake you, because you obey the voice of the Lord your God: Blessed shall you be in the city, and blessed shall you be in the country. Blessed shall be the fruit of your body, the produce of your ground and the increase of your herds, the increase of your cattle and the offspring of your flocks. Blessed shall be your basket and your kneading bowl. Blessed shall you be when you come in, and blessed shall you be when you go out. The Lord will cause your enemies who rise against you to be defeated before your face; they shall come out against you one way and flee before you seven ways. The Lord will command the blessing on you in your storehouses and in all to which you set your hand, and He will bless you in the land which the Lord your God is giving you."

    ◆ Blessings shall come upon you and overtake you, because you obey the voice of the Lord your God!
    ◆ Increase of everything you own will belong to you.
    ◆ The Lord will cause your enemies who rise against you to be defeated before your face.
    ◆ The Lord will command the blessing on you in your storehouses and in all to which you set your hand, and He will bless you in the land which the Lord your God is giving you.

What is the Holy Spirit saying to you concerning the blessings of the Lord, increase He will give you, the defeat of your enemies in front of your face, the blessing of your storehouse as well as all that you set your hand to do, and His blessing in the land that the Lord gives to you?

_____

_____

_____

What is the application concerning what the Holy Spirit is saying to you concerning the blessings of the Lord, increase He will give you, the defeat of your enemies in front of your face, the blessing of your storehouse as well as all that you set your hand to do, and His blessing in the land that the Lord gives to you?

---

2. Deuteronomy 28:11-13: "And the Lord will grant you plenty of goods, in the fruit of your body, in the increase of your livestock, and in the produce of your ground, in the land of which the Lord swore to your fathers to give you. The Lord will open to you His good treasure, the heavens, to give the rain to your land in its season, and to bless all the work of your hand. You shall lend to many nations, but you shall not borrow. And the Lord will make you the head and not the tail; you shall be above only, and not be beneath, if you heed the commandments of the Lord your God, which I command you today, and are careful to observe them."

   ◈ The Lord will grant you plenty of goods.
   ◈ The Lord will open to you His good treasure, the heavens, to give the rain to your land in its season, and to bless all the work of your hand.
   ◈ And the Lord will make you the head and not the tail.
   ◈ You shall lend to many nations, but you shall not borrow.

What is the Holy Spirit is saying to you concerning the Lord giving you plenty of goods, His opening's good treasure to give you rain in your land, His blessing of the work of your hand, His making you the head and not the tail, and His causing you to be the lender to many nations and not the borrower?

_____

What is the application the Holy Spirit is saying to you concerning the Lord giving you plenty of goods, His opening's good treasure to give you rain in your land, His blessing of the work of your hand, His making you the head and not the tail, and His causing you to be the lender to many nations and not the borrower?

_____

3. Deuteronomy 29:9: "Therefore keep the words of this covenant, and do them, that you may prosper in all that you do."

What is the Holy Spirit saying to you concerning keeping the words of the covenant and prospering in all that you do?

_____

What is the application concerning keeping the words of the covenant and prospering in all that you do?

_____

_____
_____
_____

4. Deuteronomy 30:9: "The Lord your God will make you abound in all the work of your hand, in the fruit of your body, in the increase of your livestock, and in the produce of your land for good. For the Lord will again rejoice over you for good as He rejoiced over your fathers."

What is the Holy Spirit saying to you concerning abounding in all the work of your hand, the fruit of your body, the increase of your livestock, and in your produce, and the Lord rejoice over you as He rejoices over your fathers?

_____
_____
_____
_____
_____
_____

What is the application concerning abounding in all the work of your hand, the fruit of your body, the increase of your livestock, and in your produce, and the Lord rejoice over you as He rejoices over your fathers?

_____
_____
_____
_____
_____
_____

5. Job 36:11: "If they obey and serve Him, they shall spend their days in prosperity, and their years in pleasures."

What is the Holy Spirit saying to you concerning obeying and serving the Lord and spending your days in prosperity and your years in pleasure?

_____
_____
_____
_____
_____
_____

What is the application for your life concerning obeying and serving the Lord and spending your days in prosperity and your years in pleasure?

_____
_____
_____
_____
_____

6. Proverbs 3:1-4: "My son, do not forget my law (the Word), but let your heart keep my commands; For length of days and long life and peace they will add to you. Let not mercy and truth forsake you; Bind them around your neck, write them on the tablet of your heart, and so find favor and high esteem in the sight of God and man."

What is the Holy Spirit saying to you concerning the remembrance of His Word and the keeping of His commandments in your heart in relation to length of days and peace, as well as the need for you to have mercy and truth to find favor and high esteem in the sight of God and man?

_____
_____
_____
_____
_____

What is the application concerning what the Holy Spirit is saying to you concerning the remembrance of His Word and the keeping of His commandments in your heart in relation to length of days and peace, as well as the need for you to have mercy and truth to find favor and high esteem in the sight of God and man?

_____
_____
_____
_____
_____
_____

7. Proverbs 8:32-35: "Now therefore, listen to me, my children, for blessed are those who keep my ways. Hear instruction and be wise, and do not disdain it. Blessed is the man who listens to me, watching daily at my gates, waiting at the posts of my doors. For whoever finds me finds life, and obtains favor from the Lord."

What is the Holy Spirit saying concerning your life of the blessings of those who keep God's ways, the need to hear His instruction and be wise, not to disdain it, and the importance of listening to Him, watching Him, waiting for Him, finding Him, finding life, and obtaining His favor?

_____
_____
_____
_____
_____
_____

What is the application for your life of the blessings of those who keep God's ways, the need to hear His instruction and be wise, not to disdain it, and the importance of listening to Him, watching Him, waiting for Him, finding Him, finding life, and obtaining His favor?

_____
_____
_____
_____
_____
_____

Chapter 7

Praying in the Spirit and Supernatural Provision

I thank God that I speak in tongues more than any of you.—1 Corinthians 14:18 NLT

DISCUSSION:

When I had the experience of being with Jesus for forty-five minutes in 1992, one of the most important subjects that Jesus spoke of was praying in the Spirit. Praying in the Spirit involves the yielding of your tongue to the utterance of the Holy Spirit with your spirit. God will allow you to speak mysteries from the depths of God's heart through the depths of your spirit. This activity is for your private fellowship with God. When you are in a public assembly, the gift of prophecy is more effective in building everyone up than speaking in tongues unless someone has the gift of interpretation. People must be able to understand what is being said or it is of no value to others. The apostle Paul said:

> *For if you have the ability to speak in tongues, you will be talking only to God, since people won't be able to understand you. You will be speaking by the power of the Spirit, but it will all be mysterious. But one who prophesies strengthens others, encourages them, and comforts them. **A person who speaks in tongues is strengthened personally, but one who speaks a word of prophecy strengthens the entire church**. I wish you could all speak in tongues, but even more I wish you could all prophesy. For prophecy is greater than speaking in tongues, unless someone interprets what you are saying so that the whole church will be strengthened* (1 Corinthians 14:2-5 NLT).

◆ Jesus taught me that this was the single most important activity you could engage in that would open the door to the supernatural.

◆ That is why I must discuss it often in my teaching sessions.

◆ There exists the ability to both speak in tongues and interpret them as the Spirit wills.

Yielding to the gift of prophecy and speaking the mysteries of God can be performed in your own, known language.

Remember that this activity is the way to engage the Holy Spirit in such a way that you can utter perfect prayers to the heavenly Father. Paul told the Corinthians:

> *That is what the Scriptures mean when they say, "No eye has seen, no ear has heard, and no mind has imagined what God has prepared for those who love him." But it was to us that God revealed these things by his Spirit. For his Spirit searches out everything and shows us God's deep secrets. No one can know a person's thoughts except that person's own spirit, and no one can know God's thoughts except God's own Spirit. And we have received God's Spirit* (not the world's spirit), *so we can know the wonderful things God has freely given us. When we tell you these things, we do not use words that come from human wisdom. Instead, we speak words given to us by the Spirit, using the Spirit's words to explain spiritual truths. But people who aren't spiritual can't receive these truths from God's Spirit. It all sounds foolish to them and they can't understand it, for only those who are spiritual can understand what the Spirit means* (1 Corinthians 2:8-14 NLT).

What is the Holy Spirit saying to you concerning *praying in the Spirit*?

_____

_____

_____

_____

_____

_____

_____

What is the application for your prayer life?

_____

_____

_____

_____

_____

_____

Praying out of Weakness

DISCUSSION:

I want you to know that when you pray in the Spirit out of your own inability to comprehend and perform, you are in a good position for the Holy Spirit to step in and accomplish God's will on your behalf.

- ◆ We do not always know the best way to pray.
- ◆ When you are going through a trial, you need understanding so that you can stand firm in your faith.
- ◆ God has given us help through the wonderful Holy Spirit.
- ◆ He will help you when you feel weak.
- ◆ He only wants the Father God's best for you.

This is what the apostle Paul said.

> *And the Holy Spirit helps us in our weakness. For example, we don't know what God wants us to pray for. But the Holy Spirit prays for us with groanings that cannot be expressed in words. And the Father who knows all hearts knows what the Spirit is saying, **for the Spirit pleads for us believers in harmony with God's own will**. And we know that God causes everything to work together for the good of those who love God and are called according to his purpose for them* (Romans 8:26-28 NLT).

I have found that when I yield to the Spirit of God in my weakness, He prays out the mysteries of God. The end result is that the will of God is done and everything always works out for my good. God has truly given us a powerful advocate to help us to pray more effectively.

What is the Holy Spirit saying to you concerning weakness?

_____

_____

_____
_____
_____
_____
_____

What is the application for your life?

_____
_____
_____
_____
_____

The Spirit of Truth

DISCUSSION:

*But the hour is coming, and now is, when the true worshipers will worship the Father in **spirit and truth**; for the Father is seeking such to worship Him. God is Spirit, and those who worship Him must worship in **spirit and truth*** (John 4:23-24).

Another aspect of *absolute truth* in the earth is this: the Holy Spirit was sent to us. Through this mighty member of the Trinity, we can experience the power, presence, and authority of God Himself. One of the most important things to know about the Holy Spirit is that He is the Spirit of truth. Jesus announced that the Holy Spirit was coming:

*If you love Me, keep My commandments. And I will pray the Father, and He will give you another Helper, that He may abide with you forever—**the Spirit of truth**, whom the world cannot receive, because it neither sees Him nor knows Him; but you know Him, for He dwells with you and will be in you. I will not leave you orphans; I will come to you* (John 14:15-18).

◆ We now have the Holy Spirit inside of us, and He is wanting to speak out and testify of God. So when we pray in the Spirit, we pray out the mysteries of God.

◆ Without the Holy Spirit guiding our prayers in the Spirit, we otherwise would not know how to pray perfectly.

◆ The Holy Spirit helps us to pray a perfect prayer that coordinates completely with God's Word and also with His will for our lives.

◆ The angels gather together around as we pray out the mysteries. They are not mysteries to the angels because they hear the will of the Lord as we speak forth, and they are ready to act.

◆ Remember that when we pray in the Spirit, we actually yield to the throne room of God and His authority.

And in a similar way, the Holy Spirit takes hold of us in our human frailty to empower us in our weakness. For example, at times we don't even know how to pray, or know the best things to ask for. But the Holy Spirit rises up within us to super-intercede on our behalf, pleading to God with emotional sighs too deep for words (Romans 8:26 TPT).

What is the Holy Spirit saying to you?

_____
_____
_____
_____
_____
_____
_____
_____
_____

◆ When we testify by the Spirit about Jesus, we are yielding to the Spirit of prophecy (see Rev. 19:10).
◆ We are allowing the Holy Spirit to speak absolute truth from the Throne.

*But when the Helper comes, whom I shall send to you from the Father, the Spirit of truth who proceeds from the Father, He will **testify of Me**. And you also will bear witness, because you have been with Me from the beginning* (John 15:26-27).

◆ The greatest move of the Spirit that ever will happen in the history of the world has begun. It is time for every Christian to let go of his or her life and give that life totally to God. Each Christian must make Jesus Lord over his or her entire life today.

◆ It is time to have any chains of bondage broken in every Christian's life.

◆ As every Christian yields to God, he or she releases anything that has been an anchor that keeps him or her from completely serving God.

◆ After those hindrances are gone, great things can begin to happen.

◆ Jesus had many things to say to us, but He told us that He would send the Holy Spirit to lead us into all truth. He said:

*I still have many things to say to you, but you cannot bear them now. However, when He, **the Spirit of truth, has come, He will guide you into all truth;** for He will not speak on His own authority, but whatever He hears He will speak; and He will tell you things to come.* He will glorify Me, for He will take of what is Mine and declare it to you. All things that the Father has are Mine. Therefore I said that He will take of Mine and declare it to you (John 16:12-15).

Allowing the Holy Spirit to Move upon You in Prayer

DISCUSSION:

Have you ever imagined what it was like when the "mighty rushing wind" came on the Day of Pentecost? I have, and the same type of great move of God is starting again because Heaven is visiting us in these last days. The Holy Spirit is the Master of the spirit realm. The supernatural is the Holy Spirit's everyday environment. The breath of God and the Holy Spirit are one. Jesus even breathed on His disciples one day and said, "Receive the Holy Spirit."

◆ As we learn about the mighty Holy Spirit, remember that He is to be treated as part of the Godhead.
◆ He is part of the Godhead and is expressed through wind, breath, fire, gifts, a dove, a liberator, an attorney, power, and authority—just to name a few.
◆ But remember, He is a person and part of the Holy Trinity, and He can be grieved.
◆ He is known in the Kingdom for righteousness, peace, and joy.

◆ Paul said, "For the kingdom of God is not eating and drinking, but righteousness and peace and joy in the Holy Spirit. For he who serves Christ in these things is acceptable to God and approved by men" (Rom. 14:17-18).

◆ When we pray in the Holy Spirit, we are in the Kingdom of God.

◆ The one who prays and is accepted by God serves in these three things—righteousness, peace, and joy in the Holy Spirit.

◆ When Jesus taught me to pray, He showed me that I would encounter these three attributes, as well as the *resurrection power* that raised Jesus from the dead (see Eph. 2:5).

What is the Holy Spirit saying to you concerning resurrection power?

_____

_____

_____

_____

_____

_____

_____

_____

_____

The Spirit Living in You

DISCUSSION:

When I pray under the influence of the Holy Spirit, I can sense the powers of the coming age spoken of in the book of Hebrews (see Heb. 6:5). This working of power has the ability to influence every part of your being. The mighty power will enable you to pray yourself into your answer.

◆ As you yield to the mighty Holy Spirit, He is taking you on to greater heights.

◆ These heights are where you can stand within His ability.

◆ You are able to see into the future that you could not see before moving into these heights.

◆ Your view was obstructed due to your former vantage point. He will unveil your purpose—that purpose which was recorded long ago.

◆ Your purpose was written from the Father's heart for you and now is revealed by the Holy Spirit.

◆ Yield to the Spirit of the living God and you will pray in a way that moves you into your destiny.
◆ Do not delay the entrance into the spirit realm.
◆ Pray and yield to that which the Spirit is saying.
◆ Now is the time to allow Him to pray out the mysteries of God through you!

What is the Holy Spirit saying to you about praying out the mysteries?

_____
_____
_____
_____
_____
_____
_____

Application:

_____
_____
_____
_____
_____
_____

Now is the time to allow Him to pray out the mysteries of God through you!

The Holy Spirit has the capability of raising people from the dead. He was the One who was involved in that process. Jesus told me when I had my *heavenly visitation* that He had such a relationship with the Father God and the Holy Spirit that He had to trust them when He died and went to hell. For the full account of this story, please see my previous book entitled *Heavenly Visitation*. He said with a broken voice, "I had to trust that the Father would give the command on the third day for the Holy Spirit to raise Me from the dead." The power of the Holy Spirit broke Him out of the hellish prison and brought Him back to life in His earthly body. He is the Resurrection and the Life. The Holy Spirit was the person who enabled Christ to rise to life. So when you pray, you must remember that very same power is available and effectual when we pray fervently (see James 5:16).

- ❖ We have the life of God in us.
- ❖ He wants to pray through us.
- ❖ He will quicken us.
- ❖ "The Spirit of God, who raised Jesus from the dead, lives in you. And just as God raised Christ Jesus from the dead, he will give life to your mortal bodies by this same Spirit living within you" (Rom. 8:11 NLT).
- ❖ It is time for the Holy Spirit to get our bodies energized with the life of God.
- ❖ Let faith rise up in our heart and tell our soul to trust in God.

Why are you cast down, O my soul? And why are you disquieted within me? Hope in God, for I shall yet praise Him for the help of His countenance (Psalm 42:5).

What is the Holy Spirit saying to you about being yielded to Him?

_____

_____

_____

_____

_____

_____

_____

Application:

_____

_____

_____

Being Filled with the Spirit

DISCUSSION:

It is very important to be filled with the Spirit of God. Let Him continually flow as rivers of living water out of you as you begin to pray in the Spirit (see John 7:38).

Therefore do not be unwise, but understand what the will of the Lord is. And do not be drunk with wine, in which is dissipation; but be filled with the Spirit, speaking to one another in Psalm and hymns and spiritual songs, singing and making melody in your heart to the Lord, giving thanks always for all things to God the Father in the name of our Lord Jesus Christ, submitting to one another in the fear of God (Ephesians 5:17-21).

Six characteristics of someone living a Spirit-filled life are:

1. They understand what the Lord's will for their life is.
2. They are not drunk with wine, but are filled with the Spirit.
3. They speak to one another in psalms, hymns, and spiritual songs.
4. They sing and make melody in their heart to the Lord.
5. They give thanks to their Father God.
6. They submit to one another in the fear of God.

The apostle Paul was filled with the Holy Spirit. It was a separate occasion from his salvation experience (see Acts 9:3-9). He met the Lord Christ on horseback on his way to persecute more Christians. He later had another, second experience with the Holy Spirit.

> *And Ananias went his way and entered the house; and laying his hands on him he said, "Brother Saul, the Lord Jesus, who appeared to you on the road as you came, has sent me that you may receive your sight and* **be filled with the Holy Spirit** (Acts 9:17).

From that point on, Paul spoke in tongues. He was always bold because he was filled with the Holy Spirit. He told the Corinthians, "I thank God that I speak in tongues more than any of you" (1 Cor. 14:18 NLT). Speaking in tongues is something that Jesus has told me is *the single most important activity in which a Christian can participate.* (Please see the full account on this subject in my book *Heavenly Visitation.*)

What is the Holy Spirit saying to you about being filled to overflowing?

_____

_____

_____

_____

_____

Chapter 8

The Word of the Lord and Sowing

As for God, His way is perfect; the word of the Lord is proven; He is a shield to all who trust in Him . —Psalm 18:30

DISCUSSION:

<u>2 Corinthians 9:6-8:</u> "But this I say: He who sows sparingly will also reap sparingly, and he who sows bountifully will also reap bountifully. So let each one give as he purposes in his heart, not grudgingly or of necessity; for God loves a cheerful giver. And God is able to make all grace abound toward you, that you, always having all sufficiency in all things, may have an abundance for every good work."

<u>Galatians 6:9:</u> "And let us not grow weary while doing good (sowing), for in due season we shall reap if we do not lose heart."

<u>Acts 20:32:</u> "So now, brethren, I commend you to God and to the word of His grace, which is able to build you up and give you an inheritance among all those who are sanctified."

<u>Isaiah 55:11:</u> "So shall My word be that goes forth from My mouth; it shall not return to Me void, but it shall accomplish what I please, and it shall prosper in the thing for which I sent it."

Becoming Good Soil

DISCUSSION:

When we reveal, implement, and practice our covenant with the Lord Jesus Christ in our lives, then we become attractive to Heaven. If Heaven is for you, then you must accept this as a fact. We must be people who are led by the Spirit of God so that we are actually able to have the Kingdom of God begin to work in our lives. If only we would allow the Holy Spirit to communicate this to us, we would do so much better.

On one occasion, Jesus spoke with me about the parable of the sower. I was shocked at how much I did not understand about this parable. After seeking God, I realized that this parable is concentrating on the condition of the soil and should be referred as the *parable of the soil* instead. Let us look deeply into what Jesus taught in this parable. But before we do this, I would like to quote what Jesus said about this parable from the Aramaic language, which He spoke fluently:

> *"If you're able to understand this, then you need to respond."* Then his disciples approached Jesus and asked, *"Why do you always speak to people in these hard-to-understand parables?"* He explained, ***"You've been given the intimate experience of insight into the hidden truths and mysteries of the reign of heaven's kingdom***, *but they have not. For everyone who listens with an open heart will receive progressively more revelation until he has more than enough. But those who don't listen with an open, teachable heart, even the understanding that they think they have will be taken from them"* (Matthew 13:9-12 TPT).

Wow! I can just hear Jesus saying this and letting us know that He wants us to meditate on His words until those words become so much a part of us that what He says influences every aspect of our lives.

◆ "You've been given the *intimate experience of insight* into the *hidden truths* and *mysteries* of the *reign of heaven's kingdom!*"
◆ The Spirit of God seeks out the deep things of God.
◆ "But God has revealed them to us through His Spirit.
◆ For the Spirit searches all things, yes, the deep things of God" (1 Cor. 2:10).
◆ I want to know the deep things of God.
◆ Jesus said that if we understand the parable of the sower, we have been given the deep, intimate, hidden truths and mysteries of the Kingdom of Heaven.

◈ Because we understand that God offers us such great understanding of His truths, we must respond.

What is the Holy Spirit saying to you about the deep things of God?

_____
_____
_____
_____
_____
_____
_____
_____

I have to share these truths with you because you are going to be effective in prayer and get every prayer answered when you fully understand what I am explaining.

Then He spoke many things to them in parables, saying: "Behold, a sower went out to sow. And as he sowed, some seed fell by the wayside; and the birds came and devoured them. Some fell on stony places, where they did not have much earth; and they immediately sprang up because they had no depth of earth. But when the sun was up they were scorched, and because they had no root they withered away. And some fell among thorns, and the thorns sprang up and choked them. But others fell on good ground and yielded a crop: some a hundredfold, some sixty, some thirty. He who has ears to hear, let him hear!" And the disciples came and said to Him, "Why do You speak to them in parables?" He answered and said to them, "Because it has been given to you to know the mysteries of the kingdom of heaven, but to them it has not been given. For whoever has, to him more will be given, and he will have abundance; but who- ever does not have, even what he has will be taken away from him. Therefore I speak to them in parables, because seeing they do not see, and hearing they do not hear, nor do they understand. And in them the prophecy of Isaiah is fulfilled, which says: 'Hearing you will hear and shall not understand, and seeing you will see and not perceive; for the hearts of this people have grown dull.

Their ears are hard of hearing, and their eyes they have closed, lest they should see with their eyes and hear with their ears, lest they should understand with their hearts and turn, so that I should heal them'" (Matthew 13:3-15).

Here is where we must receive the Spirit of revelation that Paul talked about in the book of Ephesians:

That the God of our Lord Jesus Christ, the Father of glory, may give to you the spirit of wisdom and revelation in the knowledge of Him, the eyes of your understanding being enlightened (Ephesians 1:17-18).

Listen as Jesus explains these truths to us. Remember that we must have "eyes that see and ears that hear."

But blessed are your eyes, because they see; and your ears, because they hear. I tell you the truth, many prophets and righteous people longed to see what you see, but they didn't see it. And they longed to hear what you hear, but they didn't hear it.

Now listen to the explanation of the parable about the farmer planting seeds: The seed that fell on the footpath represents those who hear the message about the Kingdom and don't understand it. Then the evil one comes and snatches away the seed that was planted in their hearts. The seed on the rocky soil represents those who hear the message and immediately receive it with joy. But since they don't have deep roots, they don't last long. They fall away as soon as they have problems or are persecuted for believing God's word. The seed that fell among the thorns represents those who hear God's word, but all too quickly the message is crowded out by the worries of this life and the lure of wealth, so no fruit is produced. The seed that fell on good soil represents those who truly hear and understand God's word and produce a harvest of thirty, sixty, or even a hundred times as much as had been planted! (Matthew 13:16-23 NLT)

Do you have eyes that see and ears that hear? What does this mean to you?

_____

_____

_____

_____

_____
_____
_____
_____
_____

1. *The Sower*

A farmer plants seeds. *Webster's Dictionary, 1828 Edition* defines a *sower* as "he that scatters seed for propagation. One who scatters or spreads; as a sower of words."

2. *The Seed*

The seed is the Word. According to *Webster's, seed* is "the substance, animal or vegetable, which nature prepares for the reproduction and conservation of the species. The seeds of plants are a deciduous part, containing the rudiments of a new vegetable."

3. *The Ground*

Finally, Webster defined *ground* as "the surface of land or upper part of the earth, without reference to the materials which compose it."

What is the Holy Spirit saying to you about these three terms in your life?

_____
_____
_____
_____
_____
_____
_____
_____
_____

The Four Types of Soil in Matthew 13

1. *The Footpath:*

It is very important to not only hear what God is saying, but understand it as well. Jesus, in person, wanted me to grasp truth being taught. He wanted me to take truth into my heart so that it produced a crop. Remember, it is possible to hear but walk away ***not understanding*** it. Don't let the evil one come and ***snatch away*** the Word that was planted in your heart.

2. *The Rocky Soil:*

We all have had the experience of hearing the Word of God and encountering such an awesome joy. We need to make sure that we have a depth concerning our walk with God. Our commitment level will determine our longevity during ***troubles***. When we are ***persecuted*** for believing God's Word, we will not relinquish our joy and produce a crop.

3. *The Thorns:*

Many of us are very busy concerning the affairs of this life on earth. We must not allow the Word to be crowded out by the ***worries*** of this life and the ***attraction of wealth***. The thorns are pushing out the truth of the Kingdom in your soil.

4. *The Good Soil:*

The good soil is the heart that truly receives and understands what God is saying and produces an amazing harvest, even a hundred times as much as had been planted!

The most interesting characteristic about Jesus is this: He is so simple in His approach toward truth. He gave us a sincere way to understand the way that the Kingdom of Heaven works. It is interesting to note that there is nothing to be done with the seed except to sow it.

What is the Holy Spirit saying to you about the soil of your heart?

_____
_____
_____
_____
_____
_____
_____
_____
_____

◈ The farmer sows the seed. That is what farmers do.
◈ The Lord Jesus instructed me that the seed has everything within it and is missing nothing essential to growth.
◈ A seed contains, within itself, all that is necessary for propagation.
◈ Once planted, it sprouts and produces a crop.
◈ Keep this in mind—one does not have to do anything else but just plant, water, and wait.

Every time I am speaking at a conference, I begin to minister on certain subjects concerning people's hearts through the word of knowledge. I am really ministering to their soil, which may contain rocks and thorns and other hindrances that prevent the soil's production of the Word that is sown. The Lord showed me when I came back that I should deal with the soil first, getting it ready for the sowing of the Word by ministering to the people through the word of knowledge, word of wisdom, discerning of spirits, and prophecy. He told me that if I would do this, I would see a greater harvest when I did sow the Word during the teaching time.

The teaching time occurs during the service, after this period of time. It may take ten minutes or an hour. To most people, it may seem as if I am randomly talking, but what I am really doing is getting rid of any hindrances in those who are listening so that the Word of God takes root and produces a crop in those individuals. Jesus comes and stands beside me and tells me the people's hearts. Once I know the conditions that exist, I will start to speak out on certain subjects and minister to the people en mass or individually, however God so chooses. After the Lord takes care of the issues with the people's soil, the glory will come in as I minister the Word to the people. He also tells me to speak to the staff of the church or ministry separately in a closed session. He will tell me at times to speak to the intercessory prayer group and the worship group as well in a closed session. He told me that if I could get the leadership on the same page as Him, the rest of the church or ministry would follow.

Chapter 9

The God of Favor

Favor Scriptures

Leviticus 26:9 (NIV): "I will look on you with favor and make you fruitful and increase your numbers, and I will keep my covenant with you."

Numbers 6:22-27: "And the Lord spoke to Moses, saying: "Speak to Aaron and his sons, saying, 'This is the way you shall bless the children of Israel. Say to them: "The Lord bless you and keep you; the Lord make His face shine upon you, and be gracious to you; the Lord lift up His countenance upon you, and give you peace."' "So they shall put My name on the children of Israel, and I will bless them."

Deuteronomy 23:45: "...because they hired against you Balaam the son of Beor from Pethor of Mesopotamia, to curse you. Nevertheless the Lord your God would not listen to Balaam, but the Lord your God turned the curse into a blessing for you, because the Lord your God loves you."

Psalm 5:11-12: "But let all those rejoice who put their trust in You; Let them ever shout for joy, because You defend them; Let those also who love Your name Be joyful in You. For You, O Lord, will bless the righteous; With favor You will surround him as with a shield."

Psalm 8:3-5: "When I consider Your heavens, the work of Your fingers, the moon and the stars, which You have ordained, what is man that You are mindful of him, and the son of man that You visit him? For You have made him a little lower than the angels, and You have crowned him with glory and honor.

Psalm 30:5: "For His anger is but for a moment, His favor is for life; Weeping may endure for a night, but joy comes in the morning."

Psalm 41:11: (Amplified Version) "By this I know that You favor and delight in me, because my enemy does not triumph over me."

Psalm 44:3: "For they did not gain possession of the land by their own sword, Nor did their own arm save them; But it was Your right hand, Your arm, and the light of Your countenance, Because You favored them."

Psalm 102:13: "You will arise and have mercy on Zion; For the time to favor her, Yes, the set time, has come."

Proverbs 12:2: "A good man obtains favor from the Lord, But a man of wicked intentions He will condemn."

Proverbs 14:9: "Fools mock at sin, but among the upright there is favor."

Proverbs 18:22: "He who finds a wife finds a good thing, and obtains favor from the Lord."

John 12:26: "If anyone serves Me, let him follow Me; and where I am, there My servant will be also. If anyone serves Me, him My Father will honor."

Romans 8:28: "And we know that all things work together for good to those who love God, to those who are the called according to His purpose."

Romans 8:31-32: "What then shall we say to these things? If God is for us, who can be against us? He who did not spare His own Son, but delivered Him up for us all, how shall He not with Him also freely give us all things?"

2 Corinthians 5:21: "For He made Him who knew no sin to be sin for us, that we might become the righteousness of God in Him."

Galatians 4:4: "But when the fullness of the time had come, God sent forth His Son, born of a woman, born under the law, to redeem those who were under the law, that we might receive the adoption as sons."

Ephesians 1:6: "To the praise of the glory of His grace, by which He made us accepted in the Beloved."

About Dr. Kevin Zadai

Kevin Zadai, Th.D. was called to ministry at the age of ten. He attended Central Bible College in Springfield, Missouri, where he received a Bachelor of Arts in theology. Later, he received training in missions at Rhema Bible College. He is currently ordained through Rev. Dr. Jesse and Rev. Dr. Cathy Duplantis. At age thirty-one, during a routine day surgery, he found himself on the "other side of the veil" with Jesus. For forty-five minutes, the Master revealed spiritual truths before returning him to his body and assigning him to a supernatural ministry. Kevin holds a commercial pilot license and is retired from Southwest Airlines after twenty-nine years as a flight attendant. He and his lovely wife, Kathi, reside in New Orleans, Louisiana.

OTHER BOOKS BY DR. KEVIN ZADAI

Heavenly Visitation

Heavenly Visitation Study Guide

Heavenly Visitation Prayer Guide

Days of Heaven on Earth

Days of Heaven on Earth Study Guide

Days of Heaven on Earth Prayer Guide

A Meeting Place with God

Your Hidden Destiny Revealed

Praying from the Heavenly Realms

Study Guide: Praying from the Heavenly Realms

The Agenda of Angels

The Agenda of Angels Study Guide

Salvation Prayer

Lord God,
I confess that I am a sinner.
I confess that I need Your Son, Jesus.
Please forgive me in His name.
Lord Jesus, I believe You died for me and that You are alive and
listening to me now.
I now turn from my sins and welcome You into my heart.
Come and take control of my life.
Make me the kind of person You want me to be.
Now, fill me with Your Holy Spirit who will show me how to
live for You. I acknowledge You before men as my
Savior and my Lord.
In Jesus's name.
Amen.

If you prayed this prayer, please contact us at info@kevinzadai .com for more information and material. Go to KevinZadai.com for other exciting ministry materials.

Join our network at **Warriornotes.tv**

Join our ministry training school at
WarriorNotes School of Ministry

More info at

KevinZadai.com

WARRIORNOTES
—✝— SCHOOL OF MINISTRY —➤

Let **Kevin Zadai** share with you the supernatural keys he has personally learned.

The online **School of Ministry** will help you to:

· Recognize and discern God's voice in intimate fellowship as you live out your destiny.

· Access God's healing power in order to fulfill the PERFECT plan He has for your life.

· DRIVE OUT the devil and his oppression over your life and those around you.

· Develop an experiential relationship with Jesus through heavenly visitations.

· And much more!

Enroll now for a **FREE** introductory course, ***Heavenly Visitation***!

Courses by **Dr. Kevin Zadai**

WARRIORNOTESSCHOOL.COM